CW0537022

of feathered foules,
there breeds the cheef of all,
A mighty foule, a goodlie birde,
whom men do Eagle call.
This builde her neast in highest toppe
of all the Oken tree,
Or in the craftiest place, whereof
in Irelande many bee:
Not in the bounds of Englishe pale,
whiche is a civill place,
But in the Devills Arse, a Peake
where Rebells most imbrace

from John Derricke, *The Image of Irelande* (1581) [1]

Published by Little Toller Books in 2018
Little Toller Books, Lower Dairy, Toller Fratrum, Dorset

Words © Seán Lysaght 2018

All photography © Seán Lysaght 2018 except: pages 232–233 © Egbert Polski 2018

The right of Seán Lysaght to be identified as the author of this work has been
asserted by him in accordance with Copyright, Design and Patents Act 1988

Jacket © Donald Teskey 2018

Typeset in Adobe Caslon Pro and Perpetua by Little Toller Books

Printed by TJ International, Cornwall, Padstow

All papers used by Little Toller Books are natural, recyclable products made
from wood grown in sustainable, well-managed forests

A catalogue record for this book is available from the British Library

ISBN 978-1-908213-54-9

01

Eagle Country

SEÁN LYSAGHT

A LITTLE TOLLER MONOGRAPH

To the memory of
Mattie Walsh (1921–2012)

Contents

HISTORICAL SEA EAGLE NESTING SITES

S1: MWEELREA - UGGDOL
S6: DUVILLAUN
S7: EAGLE ISLAND
S8: BARR NEAD AN IORLAIGH
S9: BENWEE HEAD
S10: PORTACLOY - SPINK
S11: PORTURLIN - PIG ISLAND
S12: PORTURLIN - LACHTMURRAGHA
S13: BENWEE - GEEVRAUN
S14: CÉIDE
S15: BELDERG - BENMORE

HISTORICAL GOLDEN EAGLE NESTING SITES

G1: ERRIFF - GLENAWOUGH
G2: ERRIFF - BEN GORM
G4: CLARE ISLAND
G5: CORRAUN
G9: COIRE NA NGARÚ

VACATED SEA EAGLE SITES OCCUPIED BY GOLDEN EAGLES

S2/G3: MWEELREA - BEN BURY
S3/G6: ACHILL - MEENAUN
S4/G7: ACHILL - SLIEVEMORE
S5/G8: ACHILL - CROAGHAUN

As I sit in the study of my house just south-west of the church at Fahy, a large window on my left gives me a view of a shallow valley, where the Moyour river winds its way among the drumlins towards Clew Bay. The top of Croagh Patrick, 'the Reek', Ireland's holy mountain, appears like a shark fin just above my neighbour's field to the right; to the left there is a ridge running east from the Reek towards Brackloon; beyond that is the ridge of the Sheeffry Hills, the coldest uplands in the area, where winter snow stays longest; then a small, nearer hill obtrudes with a section of Westport housing; and, farthest away of all in this vista, there is the flat-topped massif of Maumtrasna between the Erriff Valley and Lough Mask; finally, on the extreme left, I can just see another distant ridge of uplands, the Partry Hills, which overlook Lough Mask.

Maumtrasna attracts my view more than the overused, degraded cone of the Reek. I see it from the north-east, and I know that at the north-eastern end, Maumtrasna presents a forbidding face in the form of a large *coum* called Glenawough. The coum at Glenawough has a substantial lake of about one square kilometre: its three sides are steep and fall from about 500 metres altitude at the top to approximately 250 metres at lake level. It is one of the most impressive coums in the country, and it looks like an ideal site for one of Mayo's extinct birds, the golden eagle.

The great ornithologist Robin Ruttledge, who lived for many years at Cloonee, on the shores of Lough Carra, considered that the Erriff Valley was the last place in Ireland that held breeding golden eagles. That being the case, the ledges of the Maumtrasna massif must rank among the last places in Ireland where native golden eagles nested. When scientists were assessing possible release sites in the 1990s for a golden eagle reintroduction programme, the Mweelrea and Erriff area of south-west Mayo was a strong contender, but the project eventually opted for the Glenveagh National Park in Donegal because of the security offered by that location.

These peaks and distances are normally small considerations during the winter, set with memories of summer days walking and exploring, and with hopes of more fine days to come. For many years, my winter routines confined me to driving the small roads among the drumlins between Westport and Castlebar. There are enough of these to make Fahy famous: local folklore has it that 'there are eight roads into Fahy, but only three roads out.' Even in the era of satnav, we still get calls from delivery drivers who are having trouble finding our house.

In spring 2014, I started exploring these small country roads on foot. (My wife Jessica, who is from England, calls these winding, undulating roads 'country lanes', whereas I might use the Irish term 'boreen'.) My initial idea was to walk every public highway in the Fahy area, between the Castlebar–Newport, Westport–Newport and Westport–Castlebar roads. I had a photocopy of an Ordnance Survey map on my desk, which I gradually marked with pink highlighter pen as I recorded my coverage. I was hoping to build what writer and cartographer Tim Robinson called a 'fractal' of my experiences, equipped with a new pair of walking boots, binoculars, a notebook, and a vague, non-specialist curiosity about the place. The project was also an effort to shake off the confinement of Mayo's winter, with its challenge of storms and long nights. I was curious to see early flowers, such as barren strawberry, opposite-leaved golden saxifrage, primrose and coltsfoot in sheltered banks and ditches, and to live close to spring's unfolding calendar of migrants, such as skylark and curlew.

Walks such as these, away from approved hiking routes and the patterns of the tourist season, I soon discovered, were pretty lonely experiences. I met very few people outdoors, and those who were at home during my unscheduled, irregular excursions were probably more attentive to a TV or computer screen than to what was going on outside. But some people must have noticed me on a few occasions, as I discovered when a courteous man from the local Neighbourhood Watch scheme approached me to ask what I was doing. Another conversation with a neighbour made me realise that people were suspicious of a man – whom few of them seemed to recognise – walking the roads with a pair of binoculars. There had been burglaries in the area, and security came up as a general concern. However, once I had spoken to a few people locally and made my intentions clear, the fuss died down, and my wanderings continued.

The grey afternoons of early spring gradually delivered a small distillate of wonder: fieldfares and redwings crowded the bare trees with urgency; starlings ticked and warbled in black choirs, as if their song were a tree aflame. The streams were full during those wet weeks, and the sound of running water rose joyfully through the bare arcades of hazel and birch woodland, in a valley that I had never seen before, fewer than three kilometres from my house. Each little glen among the drumlins had a calling cock pheasant, which occasionally put in an appearance in a corner of a field, like a lost celebrity looking for a way out. I found otter spraint and prints at the foot of small stone bridges crossing the two rivers in the area, the Moyour and the Brockagh; and once, when I leaned over one of those bridge parapets, I frightened a frog into the shimmering avenue of the Brockagh and watched its yellow, naked energy crossing the dark water.

The photocopied map was steadily acquiring new pink marks recording my journeys. On one occasion my attention wandered northwards to another place: Drumilra (*Droim Iolra*, 'Eagle Ridge') was shown as a townland name to the north of the Castlebar—Newport road near the landfill site at Derrinumera. It was just outside the area I had set myself for my walking project, but the wild associations of the name were too enticing, and I decided I would have to go there to explore. Heading north of the Castlebar—Newport road meant leaving the confinement of small farms and properties in the Fahy area and entering the forestry and commonage of wild country stretching north and east towards Lough Beltra. This involved breaking away from my original plans, but I was getting restless in the narrow geography of Fahy's minor roads, and, like a restive migrant, I needed a bigger frontier.

My first foray in the direction of Eagle Ridge was a walk

north from the main road, through forestry plantation for about two kilometres. The ditches along this quiet road had a noticeable amount of rubbish from illegal dumping. All sorts of unspeakable waste was rotting in plastic bags under the pines and spruce trees, leaking effluent into the water courses. I came across the skeleton of a cow or bullock that had been dumped in the ditch and stripped clean by foxes and ravens. I failed to get the view I was hoping for that day, as my time was limited, and I had to turn back, still in the cover of conifers. The main outcome of that walk was a sense of outrage at the pollution of the Brockagh river from this part of its catchment. The Brockagh is a delightful stream which runs through a narrow limestone gorge near Fahy National School; its banks are a refuge for hazel woodland which is packed with wood anemones and bluebells in April, and it used to hold a thriving run of sea trout before the arrival of fish farming in Clew Bay.

However, it was Eagle Ridge, and not the cause of the Brockagh, that had stirred my interest, and that was the trail I would follow. In doing so, I was going back to an old interest of mine, in sea eagles and golden eagles, two species that were widespread in Mayo before their extinction in the early twentieth century. In 2001, I had travelled to Norway with Jessica and my brother Liam to see sea eagles and goshawks in the wild, and we were privileged to be shown both species on their nests. One of the best memories from that trip was stepping out of the house near Trondheim one morning to see a majestic pair of sea eagles crossing the sky; on another occasion we trekked to a sea eagle nest in a large pine tree and ringed a single chick that was soon to fledge. Liam had been involved in plans, which were then being realised, for the reintroduction of golden eagles to Ireland, and it was through his contacts that we were shown these wonderful birds. The same contacts allowed me to visit Glenveagh National Park in Donegal some months later to see the young golden eagles from Scotland being hacked back into the wild from cages hidden in woodland.

Mixing with scientists and listening to their wise conversations about eagles and eagle biology made me want to contribute something of my own. I went back to old maps and early travellers' accounts of Mayo, looking for references to eagles, and I wrote up the findings in an article, 'Eagles in Mayo: A Historical Record', which was published by the Royal Dublin Society in 2004.[2] When I showed a copy of this paper to Lorcan O'Toole, the manager of the Donegal project, he asked me if I had visited all the sites in question, and I admitted that I had not. My work had been mostly a desk-based trawl through the archive for place names, folklore references, and reports from scientists and travellers.

The idea of visiting all the mountains and sea cliffs where eagles had bred in historical times was a challenge I passed over at the time, but as my curiosity turned towards Eagle Ridge, this idea began to emerge again. Could I explore the wild territory in Mayo and identify places that held breeding golden eagles or sea eagles? I also had a hope that I might come across a wandering eagle from one of the reintroduction programmes, and so make a small contribution to an unfolding future for eagles in Mayo. So I abandoned my project of walking the lanes of Fahy for a bigger scenario: one that suited the ego of a fifty-six year old who still felt reasonably fit. Using the framework of longer days also meant that I might have a series of stories to tell, so I began to record these field days in a journal, starting with Eagle Ridge.

Eagles are now extinct in Mayo. I write this and immediately want to contradict it. If it were absolutely true, there would be no point in setting out in search of them. In my 2004 article, I wrote that both golden and [white-tailed] sea eagles are *absent* from Mayo, which does not amount to saying that they are extinct. Both species still exist, so they are not extinct, and both have been reintroduced to this island: the golden eagle in Donegal and the sea eagle in Kerry, using Scottish and Norwegian stock respectively. On the other hand, the eagles that frequented the sea cliffs and mountains of Mayo since the last glaciation were persecuted to extinction during the nineteenth century, and their genotype has been lost forever.

Since the reintroduction programmes began, eagles have turned up in Mayo on a few occasions. In November 2006, a young golden eagle (Orange 4) from the Donegal project was roosting in the Nephin Beg mountains, in the Glennamong area north of Newport. The same bird, tracked by satellite during the summer in Mayo, had then disappeared, and had returned to Mayo in the autumn for a time. On November 4, I went for a ramble in the Srahmore-Letterkeen area in the vague hope of seeing that eagle. Golden eagles in such a wild area are not normally obliging to the casual stroller, and such was the case that day. I had to be content with two ravens enjoying a mid-air romp overhead, and fieldfares, back to the winter haw fest.

In due course, a map with satellite data showed this eagle's movements between the Nephin Beg mountains in the east, and the mountains of the Corraun Peninsula in the west. The bird had an obvious preference for mountains with steep sides, such as you get in the glaciated landscapes of corries and mountain lakes in the Nephin Beg range.

Following this, in 2011, a young sea eagle from the Kerry project turned up in north Mayo, east of Lough Carrowmore. It was then reported from the Nephin Beg area generally, which meant that there was a chance of spotting it in the mountains north of Newport. This was the Srahmore district, with two lakes, Loughs Furnace and Feeagh, and plenty of water and forest, as well as rocky mountain terrain. Much of this was accessible by road to the casual Sunday afternoon driver. I was not really expecting to see anything on August 28 that year; I was simply enjoying a sense of fulfilment at the knowledge that the word 'eagle' was alive somewhere in those mountains, along with the red deer that had also returned.

Jessica and I followed our usual itinerary along Lough Feeagh, past the old youth hostel and the sporting lodge of the Stoneys from Rosturk, to the plantation at Letterkeen and the start of the Bangor trail. It was on our way back, just close to the abandoned schoolhouse at Srahmore, that I braked hard, grabbed my binoculars, and rushed out of the car to check what I knew it to be: a sea eagle, a great big lumbering frame of a bird with its wing tag, pursued by a group of ravens. The bird did not turn to challenge its pursuers, as I thought it might, but flew on urgently, with direct, purposeful beats of its huge wings, in the direction of the sea, and disappeared past the hill that overlooks the little Catholic church at Srahmore. I thought that it might have taken on one of those ravens, grabbed it in its talons to teach it who was boss of these territories, but this young eagle had a harassed look as it gave way to a local mob. And I also regretted that plastic tag it carried on its wing angle. It was a diminution of its wildness.

I had seen my first eagle in Mayo, and could make an entry in my journal, 'sea eagle at Lough Feeagh,' as if this bird's entry into literary history might somehow assist its survival. This eagle later went back to Kerry that winter, but it returned to Mayo the following March, and was frequenting the Lough Beltra area east of Newport. Then, in mid-May, the news broke that a young eagle from the Kerry project had been found dead there, having been poisoned *and* shot. I felt sadness and anger, but also an undercurrent of anticipation at the fate of this lonely, inexperienced bird wandering in areas where many shotguns are at the ready. And sea eagles, I knew, can be a more confiding species if they are not persecuted. *If.*

My journal entry for August 28, 2011, 'sea eagle at Lough Feeagh', was less than a year old when it became history, and as I look at it again, it stands alongside all those other eagle records from the late nineteenth and early twentieth centuries, of birds trapped, poisoned or shot. As Robert Lloyd Praeger chronicled the demise of eagles in Ireland, in *The Way that I Went* (1937), he mentioned a golden eagle that was seen on the north Mayo coast in the early 1930s, and a young sea eagle shot on Clare Island in 1935. He concluded, 'One would like to hope that this is not the last that will be seen in Ireland of either of these grand creatures: but considering the reception that usually awaits them and others, it might be kinder to hope that neither eagle will again visit our country. In Scotland, under wise protection, the golden eagle is more than holding its own; but heaven help the bird that ventures near the "Island of Saints".'[3]

With its own rich history of eagles, and two active eagle reintroduction programmes, Mayo stands between the past and the future as an eagle territory. The past is marked, in the first instance, by eagle references in Irish place names, particularly along the north Mayo coast from Erris Head to Céide. There is a 'green of the eagle' on a headland east of Belderg harbour (*Scraith an Iolra*, G 003421), and an 'eagle rock' nearby (*Carraig an Iolra*, G 003420). An entire valley, *Gleann Iolra*, south-east of Céide (G 005391), derives its name from the eagle, as does the river that flows through the glen. Four kilometres south of Belderg, a hill with a cliff face above a mountain lake is known locally as Eagle Rock (F 998353). A headland near Benwee Head, 'the peak of the eyrie' (*Barr Nead an Iorlaigh*, F 792413), tells us that eagles used to breed there. Erris Head has a 'crag of the eagle' (*Speanc an Iolra*, F 715396), and off the west coast of the Mullet there is Eagle Island.

Farther south, in the mouth of Clew Bay, Clare Island has an 'eagle peak' on its north coast (L 693881). A low hill on Killary Harbour, near the mouth of the Bundorragha River, is called 'eagle crag' (*Screig an Iolra*, L 845631). Mount Eagle is a hill east of Srahmore in the Nephin Beg range (G 004044); the same range of mountains has *Carraig an Iolra* ('eagle rock', F 956046) on a hillside north of Lough Feeagh, 'eagle's nest' on a steep incline above Glendahurk (F 909026), and *Screig Iolra* ('eagle crag', F 902183) on the northern slope of Maumykelly near Bangor.[4] Closest of all to where I live is *Droim Iolra* ('eagle ridge'), six kilometres east of Newport (M 032939).

These Irish place names are corroborated in literature by

many occasional references and a few extended descriptions. W. H. Maxwell, who had a keen eye for such things, described sea eagles in the Doo Lough Valley hunting for salmon, in *Wild Sports of the West* (1832):

> They chose a small ford upon the rivulet which connects Glencullen with Glendullagh, and posted on either side, waited patiently for the salmon to pass over. Their watch was never fruitless, and many a salmon, in its transit from the sea to the lake, was transferred from his native element to the wild eyrie on the Alpine cliff, that beetles over the romantic waters of Glencullen.[5]

Edward Newman reported that sea eagles were 'very abundant' on Achill in 1838, and the same abundance of eagles and ravens on Achill impressed Mr and Mrs Hall at about the same time. Caesar Otway, whose travel books are a rich source of eagle lore, was struck by the numbers of eagles he saw near Benwee Head on the north Mayo coast about 1840: 'I never saw so many of these birds at one time, except at Horn Head [Donegal].'[6] Other excursionists such as John Hervey Ashworth and Charles Weld described sea eagles on Achill in the 1850s, and these birds enter romantic iconography with their references to 'sublime scenery', and how a pair at Keem took off and 'both majestically soared aloft towards the inaccessible cliffs of Minnaane'.[7] However, not everything was grandly sublime in these landscapes. Maxwell, a sportsman of the old school, reported that sea eagles at Slievemore on Achill were a nuisance around Doogort, taking geese and hens. George Roper, who wrote *A Month in Mayo* (1876), thought that the sea eagle was 'a lazy gluttonous bird', justly persecuted by the farmer because of its liking for lambs. In her memoir of life in the Doo Lough Valley, *Twenty Years in the Wild West* (1879), Mrs Matilda Houstoun described the destruction of a family of eagles at a nest above Doo Lough.

As you follow the chronicle of eagles in Mayo through the late nineteenth century, you get a heartbreaking litany of destruction. As early as 1850, on a visit to Castle Taylor in County Galway, the naturalist A. G. More was talking about the 'extermination' of the eagles in the west with his hosts, the Shawe-Taylors. Even the ornithologist Robert Warren shot a pair of sea eagles at Bartragh, on Killala Bay, on December 4, 1851. By 1876, George Roper believed that the spread of 'the grouse disease' in Mayo was due to the destruction by gamekeepers of 'the hawks, buzzards and harriers, which *formerly* abounded on the bogs and moors'.[8] As well as gamekeepers and proto-scientists, there were also trophy hunters taking eggs and young, so that by the late nineteenth century the situation had become critical.

As the ornithologist Richard James Ussher gathered information on Ireland's birds, an informant on Achill told him in 1880 that he had 'known six [eagles] in one week fall victim to poison.' The same correspondent, J. R. Sheridan, wrote to Ussher in 1891 that he remembered the mission keeper at Dugort 'to have poisoned eleven Golden Eagles in one year.'[9] The Ussher papers, preserved at the Royal Irish Academy in Dublin, also tell a story of relentless persecution of a pair of golden eagles at a traditional nest site in the Erriff Valley, possibly Ben Gorm.

When Ussher and Warren published their *Birds of Ireland* in 1900, Ussher thought that the sea eagle was 'on the point of extinction' in Ireland, with perhaps a single pair left on the cliffs of the north Mayo coast. Breeding continued at this site, between Portacloy and Porturlin, for at least six years, but Ussher was unable to find evidence of breeding when he visited in 1910.

The golden eagle was also headed towards the same fate, although it did hold out longer. There were golden eagles at a number of Mayo locations up to about 1911, in the Erriff Valley, on Achill, and in the Nephin Beg mountains. Robin Ruttledge knew of breeding in the Erriff Valley up to 1912,[10] and Harry Scroope told Ussher in 1912 that 'eagles are often seen in the Corslieve [Nephin Beg] mountains',[11] but this claim seems an exaggeration. There is one record of a golden eagle from Buckoogh, in the east of the range, from 1911.[12] The last record of the golden eagle on Achill is March 1911.[13] Praeger mentions a single golden eagle that was seen around the north Mayo coast up to 1931 as the last eagle in Mayo, and possibly the last in Ireland. The last one in Donegal had been trapped in 1926.[14]

And so, apart from a Scottish pair that bred on the north Antrim coast for a few years in the fifties, native Irish and Mayo eagles pass into the otherworld of history and taxidermy. A mounted golden eagle in private ownership in Westport, County Mayo, is supposed to be 'the last eagle on Achill', but it carries no date. The golden eagle preserved in the Natural History Museum in Dublin was killed on Clare Island in 1887. The last Mayo golden eagle that I know of is a preserved specimen, now at the visitors' centre in Glenveagh National Park, which was shot at Bangor Erris in 1915.

Now our hopes for Mayo eagles rest on birds visiting from Donegal and Kerry, where they have been reintroduced, or on wanderers from western Scotland. The golden eagle reintroduction programme in Donegal started in 2001, with the first instance of successful breeding in 2007. Since then, there has been a precious chronicle of chicks reared most years. Most of the breeding success in Donegal has been in the Glenveagh area, where the rangers of the National Park can keep an eye on the eyries. After some setbacks, including cases of poisoning and of clutches lost owing to wet summers, people in Donegal are now hoping that a small population of seven or eight territorial pairs can be established between the Glenveagh area and the Blue Stack mountains.

At the moment, with the low rate of recruitment of juveniles, the idea of eagles spreading from territories in Donegal is a distant prospect, but still a possibility. Golden eagles are mostly sedentary, but young birds can wander within a radius of 150 kilometres, as was the case with Orange 4, which visited the Nephin Beg mountains in November 2006.

The outlook for sea eagles is different. Since the reintroduction programme started in Kerry in 2007, it is noticeable how widely these birds have dispersed. Satellite tracking shows that a young sea eagle can roam the length of the island of Ireland in a few days. One of the named birds, Star, flew from Killarney to Mullaghmore, County Sligo, within the first two weeks after its release in August 2009. Zanzi, a great wanderer, was tracked from Kerry to Fermanagh and back in autumn 2012, and flew through Mayo on its journey home. (There is a GPS fix of Zanzi near Manulla, south of Castlebar, on October 9, 2012.) A group of three sea eagles were seen at Altnabrocky in the Nephin Beg mountains in May 2015. And to add to these official records, several years ago I got a phone call from an English couple living near Céide who gave me an account of a very large raptor they had seen during a period of stormy weather that winter. From the details they provided, I concluded at the time that they had seen a juvenile sea eagle.

Following the first successful breeding attempt in 2013, sea eagles bred successfully at five sites in four counties, Cork, Kerry, Clare and Galway, in 2016. They have shown a preference for densely wooded sites near water, and there are many such places in Mayo where this species might settle in the future.

All this leads me to have more hopes of meeting *Haliaeetus albicilla* (white-tailed sea eagle) than *Aquila chrysaetos* (golden eagle) on a day out in Mayo. In addition to birds wandering from the current breeding territories, there is a strong chance of a sea eagle from Scotland turning up on the Mayo coast. There are currently about a hundred territories in western Scotland following two reintroduction programmes, and a third programme is underway in eastern Scotland. The eagle my informants at Céide had seen may well have been a Scottish bird. One hundred and eight years after Ussher described the last sea eagles in Mayo, the cliffs between Erris Head and Céide are ready to receive visitors again.

But now he knows these hills, that is to say
he knows them better, and if ever again he
sees them from afar it will be I think with
other eyes, and not only that but the within,
all that inner space one never sees, the brain
and heart and other caverns where thought
and feeling dance their sabbath, all that too
quite differently disposed.

Samuel Beckett, Molloy

April

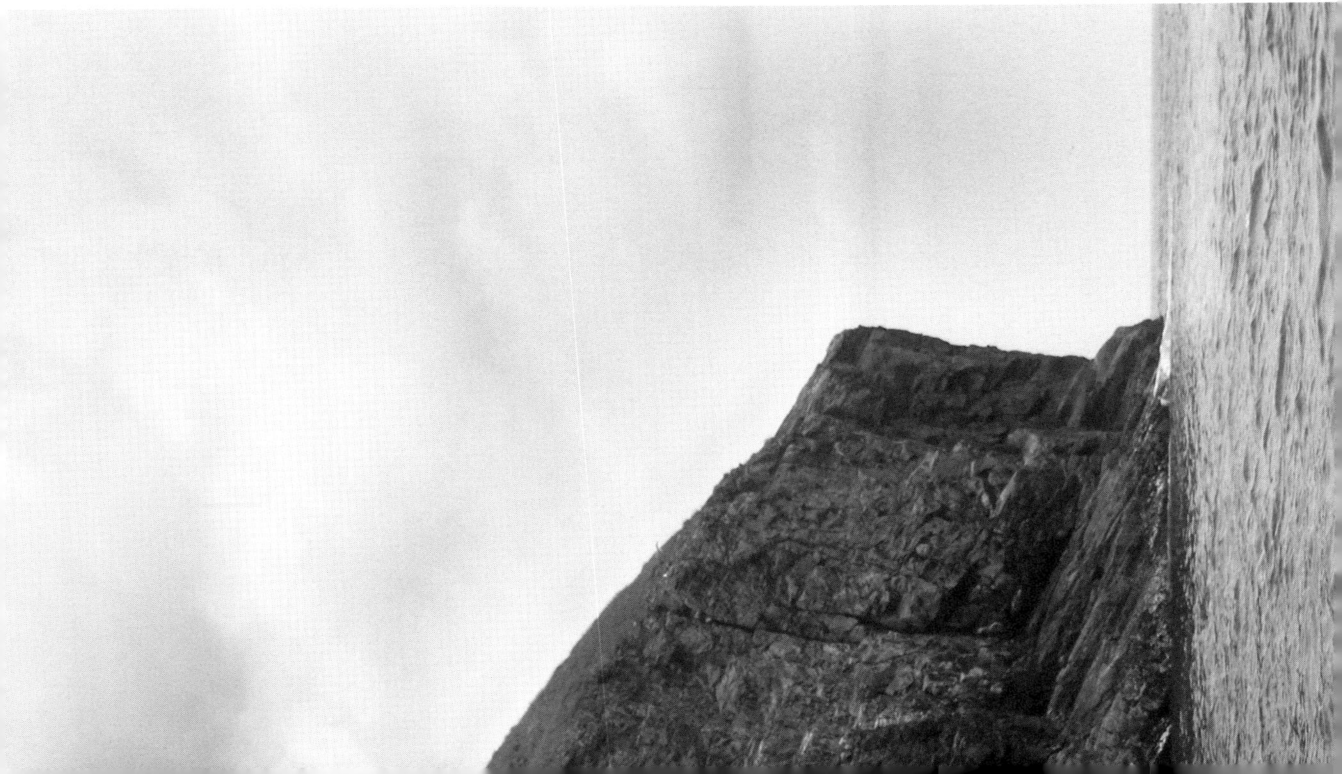

Eagle Ridge

April 17

I approached Drumilra from the north, in an area of wild, open country with some forestry plantations. One of these, on the southern slope of Buckoogh (pronounced 'buck-a'), is like the profile silhouette of Wolfe Tone, the leader of the 1798 rebellion. I parked near a gate overlooking Beltra Lough and set out along a moorland track towards Derrinumera and Drumilra. One of the rare western Irish heathers, *Erica mediterranea*, was still in flower on the bog at the end of its winter season, while the new growth on willows along the plantation edges were yellow-green sponge dabs of brightness. A song thrush was singing.

As I walked, a flock of sheep moved ahead of me along the track – they are the walker's constant companions in the bogs and mountains of the west, and during my searches even the most remote corries continually echoed to the sounds of bleating sheep. I also noticed a flock of feral goats browsing among the willows on cutaway bog: these animals make distinctive marks by eating the bark of willows and their traces were everywhere on the trees lining the plantation margins.

A right-hand track took me towards the old landfill at Derrinumera, which was once so teeming with gulls and crows that a falconer was employed to scare the birds off and destroy the pastime of the birders who used to come here looking for rare gulls. Nowadays, the rubbish is shaped into a grassy plateau with various pipes and outlets for methane, and a pond for leachate. Thirteen ravens occupied the site when I arrived: Eagle Ridge had been upstaged by Raven Plateau.

The path to Eagle Ridge led through another gate along the plantation. The stony track faded away to a sheep trail, in places saturated and full of sphagnum. On some of the drier stretches, ling heather (*Calluna vulgaris*), black bog rush and dwarf willow had gained a foothold. A second gate on the left took me into a firebreak in the plantation. A strong breeze picked up and washed my face as the track rose and faced south-west. A digger worked somewhere in the distance.

When I emerged onto the top of Eagle Ridge, I saw the concrete trig point 200 metres away on the horizon. The drumlins between Newport and Westport were spread out to the south, a landscape of shallow green hills, like a voluptuous body asleep. These drumlins continued into Clew Bay, where the sea has flooded the hollows between them, creating many small islands of a 'drowned drumlin' complex; according to tradition, there is one of these islands for every day of the year.

This was the view I savoured, without going any farther. A barbed-wire fence separated me from the last section of the ridge, where the noise of a working Hymac prevailed. I am shy in such situations, and the sight of a stranger approaching across such an unfrequented horizon would have raised suspicions. Over thirty years ago, during a trip to the Isle of Skye, a friend and I traipsed up a hill to a similar trig point and found golden eagle feathers left by a preening bird.

I listened to birds singing in the plantation on either side of the firebreak as I sat in the heather eating figs and chocolate: robin, chaffinch, willow warbler, blackbird and wren. They sounded the same as the species in my garden, although the location was so different. Along with these, I had the ghosts of eagles past, soaring on the updraughts off that hill in days before any of it was forested, and Eagle Ridge gave the eagle eye a commanding prospect of wild countryside and mountain, from the proud mass of Nephin in the east, to the pyramid of Croagh Patrick in the west.

The view to the north looks over Beltra Lough to the Nephin Beg chain of mountains including Nephin, Birreencorragh and Buckoogh. On that first day, my eye was drawn to the scree falls under Birreencorragh, and I decided to continue my exploration there. Then I sent a text to my wife, 'On my way back from Eagle Ridge.' 'OK, cowboy,' was her reply.

Mount Eagle
April 25

I walked into the glen between Buckoogh and Birreencorragh, along the Skerdagh river, to check approaches and access to the latter mountain, just a fathom short of 700 metres high. Like most glens in the Nephin Beg range, this is forestry ground, alternating with blanket bog and sheep country. In late April, young birch plantings were a delicate, pale green, the colour of spring. These occasional stands of broadleaves among the regimented lines of conifers have tempted migrant warblers into these areas: blackcaps and grasshopper warblers were singing in the younger plantings.

At one point along this track, where spruce trees cast long shadows, I came face to face with an abandoned house and the dark, empty sockets of its door and window openings. The rendered walls said that this house was lived in up to the mid-twentieth century; there was no sign of an electricity cable, so the people here kept their winter vigil by candlelight and lamplight. Ruins like this, monuments to the decline of hill communities, always obtrude against the walker's nature love. I passed on, and discovered a flooded section of track more to my liking: a small stream running across the surface with a series of shallow pools full of tadpoles and pond skaters – Yeats's 'long-legged flies', ripe for insight.

The forestry track did not end at the house, as the map suggested, but carried on to the ford, and so joined the trail that ringed Buckoogh to the west. This was a detail that I would save for another day. The riverbank around the ford was rich with signs of otters: little runs and tracks along the grassy bank, punctuated by dark spraint.

After a couple of hours, pottering around like this, savouring the time of year, and checking the ascent of Birreencorragh, I got back to the car and discovered from the map that the peak at the top of the glen, directly in line with my walk, was Mount Eagle. I had noticed the name many times before on the OS map, but had forgotten about it as I was thinking about Birreencorragh.

As I approach my house, coming from Westport, Mount Eagle is one of a number of summits in the Nephin Beg range that line up ahead of me. When I turn off the main Westport–Castlebar road to take the road to Fahy, I see the 808-metre peak of Nephin, to the east of the range. After a couple of kilometres, a subtle swing in the road brings Buckoogh into line, and a little farther on, I have Birreencorragh on the horizon. This peak is set in a cluster of supporting ridges: Mount Eagle forms the shoulder of one of these on the western side, its peak like a decorated epaulette.

This shifting, reassembling range of mountains is a lesson in perspective; as many experienced walkers know, mountains have a habit of hiding behind others, of fading away under ridges, only to reveal themselves in a few moments to the walker, presenting facets and angles that were never apparent before, and which no map can ever capture. Their bulk and permanence belies the ability of mountains to shift or sink, to fade away and be rediscovered in new light and vastness. Sometimes this is an effect of light and atmosphere; at other times it is we ourselves, constantly moving, forgetting as well as looking, who are responsible for the versatility of the horizon. And so, that day, as I looked down at otter spraint and pond skaters in that valley, the colossus of Mount Eagle loomed to the south without my noticing.

Birreencorragh
April 27

Following the route I had established two days earlier, I started the climb from the south, at Skerdagh, and walked up a long, gradual spur towards a first eminence at 340 metres. Beltra Lough gradually came into view above the conifers, and the Reek had a wisp of cloud, like stray, uncombed locks.

The drumlin islands of Clew Bay were spread all over the south-west.

By 8.30 a.m., I had reached a fence at about 300 metres and saw that the ground beyond it was heavily grazed by sheep, a legacy of the farming free-for-all in these uplands. The western Irish uplands are associated in most people's minds with wildness, but they are in fact heavily marked by overgrazing; it does not take a botanist's eye to notice that the ground vegetation has been transformed over wide expanses. The slopes approaching Birreencorragh from Skerdagh are the standard yellow-green colour of degraded ground, a combination of mat grass (*Nardus stricta*), deer sedge (*Trichophorum cespitosum*), purple moor grass (*Molinia caerulea*), and various species of sphagnum moss. The rich brown tone of heather is in places confined to inaccessible slopes and gullies, or to privately owned areas that have been fenced off by landowners. On the badlands of overgrazed terrain, hares and red grouse are rarities, and these two species are a vital ingredient in the diet of golden eagles, especially as live prey for young eagles during the breeding season.

All this is a result of the explosion in sheep numbers during the 1990s under the European Union's Common Agricultural Policy. In 1992, the national ewe flock peaked at 4.8 million, not far off double the current number. By the end of that decade, the deterioration of the western uplands was so severe that the European Court of Justice examined the situation and eventually, in 2002, condemned Ireland for 'allowing serious deterioration of wild-bird habitats to occur through overstocking by sheep'. In 2004, the European Commission decided to pursue infringement proceedings against Ireland for nine breaches of environmental law. The situation was especially severe in remoter parts of the west, and the Commission's case against Ireland focussed in particular on the plight of red grouse in the Owenduff/ Nephin Beg Special Protection Area (SPA) in north Mayo, just a few minutes west of Birreencorragh as the eagle flies.

With the full machinery of EU sanctions ranged against it, the Irish government was forced to act, and in 2006 the National Parks and Wildlife Service (NPWS) reached an agreement with farmers in the SPA: sheep would be removed during November and December, and again from mid-February until mid-May. This was a first step in reversing a situation that had stripped many upland areas of Mayo of its vegetation; in the worst affected areas, overgrazing and trampling had transformed entire hillsides into dreary wastes of exposed peat.

With a high level of compliance by farmers, the NPWS was subsequently able to show that the process had been arrested, vegetation was recovering, and the population of red grouse had increased. A major field survey of red grouse in the Owenduff/Nephin Beg area in 2012 reported a doubling of numbers to between 790 and 832 birds, compared with a population low, in 2002, of 362 to 426 individuals.[15] By then, the Commission had decided to close its case against Ireland over breaches of EU habitats legislation.

In recent years, there has been some lifting of restrictions in areas of Mayo where habitat has recovered, but in much of Mayo's eagle country, the walker still meets the desolation of overgrazing. The national park area in the northern part of the Nephin Beg mountains is one where the NPWS has most control, and you can count on meeting a few grouse on an average day's excursion; but to the south of the range grazing controls are still in place because the ground is 'knackered', as one ranger put it to me.

The desertification of the Irish uplands makes any sound of life special: that day there were a few, distinct in the stillness: the lonely bleating of a lamb, the song of skylarks, the call of a cuckoo. The summit of the Reek was now clear of cloud.

When I reached the 340-metre point, there was a sudden vista to the north: scree on the slopes of Glendorragha, a deep glen right under the main summit, embraced by two ridges, one of which I was climbing, and crags on the western slopes of Mount Eagle. Farther out to my right, the Paul Henry massif of Nephin formed a sublime horizon, a kind of blue-grey essence of distance, a single tone of dark colour. To the west, Buckoogh presented a substantial cliff in the coum overlooking Lough Nambrackkeagh. The Skerdagh river below me was a silver vein twisting over the valley floor.

Then I saw a shape on the horizon above, resolving itself into two walkers, and I felt that I had lost my fantasy of solitude and discovery. (*The Irish Times* had just conducted a poll to find the wildest county in Ireland, and by far the biggest vote went to Mayo, so finding others on this mountain was hardly surprising.)

As I rested at 450 metres, there were veils of cloud drapery over the peaks to the north-west; the vast stone ridges of Glennamong divided the wide catchment of the Owenduff river in Erris from Clew Bay to the south. In these perspectives, there seemed to be more mountain than lowland, dwarfing the plain where we spent most of our time.

After about 500 metres elevation, the ground became truly montane: boulders were covered in a military-green moss, with rusty leaves of bilberry coming through. There were signs of ferocious exposure; rocks seemed to be melting away, leaving the quartz bands in relief. Long scree falls draped the great bowl of Glendorragha to my right, and a chocolate-brown colour on the upper slopes suggested heather cover for grouse, but there were no cliffs or crags that looked suitable for an eyrie.

I set off along the dorsal spine of the ridge, following an old boundary line of stones between the first and second of three cairns. The ground was nearly level along the top of the ridge at about 550 metres, with the rocky cone of Birreencorragh ahead. Then I came across large peat hags where the peat was up to two metres deep, exposed at the sides. The green turf-tops were like the crests of waves breaking over the peat slopes. In places, the peat resembled the front of a glacier creeping across the ridge. And in one spot, the vegetation cover had gone completely, leaving a shallow barrow of peat framed by a margin of silvery rock fragments between it and the sward, like an Andy Goldsworthy or Richard Long creation. Plenty of flies were about in the lee of these banks, allowing the meadow pipit to scratch a living. His thin 'sip' at the silence was the only sound.

A rectangular dip in the ground had filled with water and lime-green sphagnum. Following all the dry weather, the water had reduced, so that the green quilt of moss was sunk a little into the rectangular trench, as if someone had thrown a fabric over the trench to cover it. The result was a pleasing unity of colour and form.

A scramble over loose stones, very like the ascent of the Reek, took me to the top of Birreencorragh and here I met the two others, experienced hillwalkers from Castlebar. It was surprisingly hot in the sheltered side of the cairn, where we chatted over sandwiches, with a few midges gathering. The trig point behind us had been split by lightning and lay across the cairn in fragments; a second cairn close by was arranged like a bowl, with a hollow inside for some ritual of love or initiation.

'There are three springs off the mountain,' said one of the men, pointing towards a forestry plantation on the northern side of Mount Eagle. 'You have to mix water from all three, and that's a cure for kidney stones. I brought fifteen litres of it back to a man on Achill, but he said it did not cure him and he had to have them out anyway.' He followed this with another story about taking a quantity of this water to a sick horse, which eventually died. 'It didn't die of thirst, anyway,' said the other. The frail spindrift of words dispersed and we contemplated the Nephins in the unusual heat. Eventually, the midges became a nuisance and we left; I allowed the other two to descend ahead of me, back to the first ridge, and struck out on my own for Mount Eagle.

Another group of walkers on their way up the ridge were calling to each other and posing for a camera. I waved a greeting to them as they went up, with no words exchanged. My tinnitus had cleared; it was hot, too hot to rest in any comfort, so I traipsed along one more green-yellow whaleback at about 500 metres before a slow descent to Mount Eagle (427 m). Birreencorragh's eastern extension was spread to my right, rock-and-scree silvery, like the shoulders of a great bull.

I decided to avoid the top of the intervening hill and skirt its side. On my way across I had to negotiate a steep, almost vertical slope at the head of the valley, the first time on this walk that I had been at all challenged by a drop, let alone a cliff. The terrain was too rounded for an eyrie. I kept going towards Mount Eagle in the hope of more dramatic contours, with a raven calling overhead.

A gentle slope took me down towards the saddle. From this perspective, Mount Eagle was a dull, flat-topped hill, about the shape of a stranded jellyfish. A rusted, decaying sheep fence became my guideline; the effect of rust was to make the wire disintegrate as if it were melting, and there were traces of an old drainage ditch running away at right angles. I am always amazed at the labour that was expended in these desolate places decades ago, and how the signs of all that effort are still visible everywhere in these hills, so many variations on what, in *The Woodlanders*, Thomas Hardy called 'Unfulfilled Intentions'.

The noise of engines reached me from the plantation to the north, as if a group of youngsters were racing trail bikes along the tracks. The noise set me smiling again at the vanity of my own wish to escape. After an interval, the sounds faded, and next thing a shape appeared briefly on the flank of Mount Eagle – I imagined a deer, perhaps a descendant of the herd that was released some years ago to the north of these mountains, and had now spread throughout the range, assisted by the shelter of forestry. The dream was dispelled a moment later when two quad bikes emerged on the top of my destination; each of them had a passenger clinging to the driver; I watched them dismount to admire the view – my view! I watched a wheatear flitting about on the boulders as my amusement rose and dispersed.

Then, as if by some kind of reward, I looked down to discover a dark, perfectly still *lochán* fifty metres by eight at the top of the valley where the plantation started. This was close to the point that my companion indicated when he spoke about the three springs, and I felt sure that this calm eye of the mountain was the source, not just of water, but of stories of cures. As the quads descended towards the exposed, peaty ground to my right, one of them got stuck in the mire and I felt the onset of schadenfreude before I continued to the top of the hill. On a tight sward of moss, a few stones were gathered into a cairn to mark the summit of Mount Eagle; I heard a cuckoo calling over two kilometres away at Srahmore, in the next valley to the west.

The heat had now become a real burden, because I was wearing and carrying too much stuff, thinking that late April would still be chilly in the uplands. As there was nowhere to shelter, I kept going down the slope, still looking for that elusive eyrie cliff. I saw crags and boulders, but nothing on the scale that I had imagined. Eventually, succumbing to exhaustion, I found a shelter the size of a cave mouth under an overhang where I could stretch out, under a roof of rock. I got rid of boots and a few layers, and cooled my skin in the sun. I thought of Praeger, who was defeated only by heat on a few occasions during his long career tramping across the countryside in search of plants.

I eventually roused myself to go down the steep slope to the valley bottom, where the Skerdagh river gathers water from Buckoogh and the broad flank of Birreencorragh to form a lively stream. Even after weeks without rain, this stream from the deep core of the mountains was still chuckling with long memories of wet weather.

I found a dead sheep in one of the abandoned fields of the valley, with its fleece still intact and another sheep skeleton nearby which had been picked clean by scavengers. This explained why ravens were quartering the valley as I made my way down. I wondered if this were a sheep cemetery where ailing sheep went to die, or if this were where the farmer left dead animals as an air burial for scavengers. It was difficult to see how an animal could have been brought here and dumped, given the nature of the terrain. I thought of a sick animal making its own way there to surrender its life.

As I walked past, noticing the empty eye sockets, I was shocked to realise that the animal was still alive: its nostrils twitched and it was still breathing. A fly walked across the rim of its eye. It was too weak to bleat or protest, but its body was still operating. Perhaps out of squeamishness or negligence, I did not intervene, but passed on. Nor did I linger at a ruined cottage nearby.

If a farmer had brought the animal here, why should he object to an eagle coming down to have its portion of carrion? I added the bird in my imagination to the list of scavengers that would soon be tussling and haggling over this animal's carcass. I wanted the eagle's great bulk to outdo the raven in size and priority at the scavengers' feast, and I wondered if the day would come when a sea eagle would quarter this valley in its search for food.

If that happened, the eagle would face the threat of poisoning: poisoned meat can easily be left in remote places such as this with the intention of killing foxes, hooded crows and magpies, if not eagles. Although illegal, this practice still goes on; toxicology results for sea eagles poisoned in Ireland have shown that nitroxynil, the active ingredient in Trodax, is the commonest toxin. Trodax is a legally available fluke drench for sheep, but it can also be put into a carcass to poison scavengers; and there are some sheep farmers, I am told, who are still absolutely determined to control vermin in this way. Anyway, the dying sheep was a poor sacrifice on my altar to the eagle. Such casualties can keep adult eagles fed during the winter, but they are no substitute for smaller, live prey during the nesting season.

I followed the stream on its way to becoming the Skerdagh river, stepping over a succession of little streams coming off the flank of the ridge that had taken me up to Birreencorragh that morning. With forest on both sides of me, I was grateful that the foresters had kept the riverbank open, and I picked my way along an avenue of birdsong, following the otter's grassy spoor.

Mount Eagle continued to perplex me: why the name, if there were no suitable eyrie sites? And what about the shelf I had crawled into to escape the sun? Could that not have been an ideal eyrie site? The threat of foxes and other ground predators said otherwise. I now believe that Mount Eagle was not a nest site, but a favourite spot for eagles to perch and preen, and enjoy the updraught. Eagles nesting on Buckoogh three kilometres away could have left their sheltered corrie, where the prevailing winds were not favourable, and crossed the valley in a brief glide. Prevailing winds rising up against the steep, west-facing slope of Mount

Eagle would have given them the lift they needed to set out on hunting forays across the entire range, eastwards over Birreencorragh or westwards, towards the peaks surrounding Glennamong. The golden eagle that was tracked to Mayo in 2006 had been recorded at Mount Eagle; this confirms an old adage of the eagle watcher: 'Once an eagle rock, always an eagle rock.'[16]

Ben Gorm – Glennamong
May 14

I drove TO Srahmore in the afternoon to check a crag on the side of Ben Gorm. The road took me around the top of Lough Feeagh, into Glennamong, a heavily forested valley cradled by a horseshoe of ridges. I approached the plantation under the bulwark of *Torc Shléibhe* (401 m), which guards the mouth of this valley. I parked just before the old concrete footbridge, crossed the river and skirted the plantation. Bluebells and pignut were in flower. From there it was a long stroll up the corrie. Huge blocks of rock fallen from the cliff overhead littered the bowl of the corrie, its outer rim shaped by a terminal moraine like a great rampart above the river. I found a few old grouse droppings, and the higher slopes looked well clad in heather: the species must be recovering here, as it had at Srahduggan on the other side of the mountains.

I scanned the rock to see if there was a suitable ledge, but it did not look promising. A mossy face ran into the fold of the cliff, too steep to support a large nest. The only inaccessible ledges were thin seams of green, which might suit guillemots in a coastal location, but would not do for an eagle. Besides, if this rock face had any decent ledges, you would expect a peregrine or a raven to be about the place, but there was nothing, just the sound of a stream splashing onto rock somewhere.

There are not many places where the landscape is so raw and elemental, as if the glacier had only recently passed by. A small lake lies at a slightly lower level to the south, and this I glimpsed before I turned to go. Bluebells were in flower in small cups and hollows, a sign that this area was once wooded. A ridge running off the southern side of Ben Gorm is known locally as Oghilles (pronounced 'o-hilly', from *eochailli*), meaning 'yew woods'. If the area is completely bereft of tree cover now, there was woodland here once, and the ancestors of these bluebells may have appeared in spring under a canopy of yews.

Leaving the corrie and crossing the lip of the moraine, I heard water running underground among the rocks. The large blocks were covered with peat and sward, but the water had kept channels open under them, so as I walked I was following the beginnings of a stream draining out of the corrie and heading down the slope that I had just climbed. Lovely lush growth of bilberry and St Patrick's cabbage was preserved in the gaps between the boulders where browsing sheep could not reach. All the time the noise was a reminder of open channels under my feet – and a possibility that at any moment the ground might give way and my leg be swallowed by hollow ground. I was thankful to have a fully charged mobile phone in my pocket.

Some distance farther down, the water emerged in places into lively glimpses of fresh streams across dark stones that ran away again into peaty sward. I stopped for a drink of water, thinking that, as it ran underground, it would not be heavily polluted with sheep droppings and urine, as was the case with other mountain brooks. After another stretch of hidden existence, the water re-emerged. The river's course became a narrow corridor of rushes growing on the silt thrown up by this tiny river; then, as it emerged again, it divided in two, and flowed back together (like the dividing and conjoined Seine in Samuel Beckett's *Ohio Impromptu*) around a succession of peat hags with scruffy hairdos of sedge and mat grass, miniature versions of the peat hags on the ridge near Birreencorragh.

Eventually, after a couple of hundred metres of being a small-scale river, with cascades, pools and even deposits of gravel, this course of water surrendered part of its flow to a length of black piping and a small concrete tank at the edge of the plantation. Local knowledge and skill had been here long before me, and set up a reservoir for a water scheme.

A few plants of heath spotted orchid appeared on the bog as I came back down.

Glennamong
May 22

Lough Feeagh was blurred by showers on my second visit. A brilliant, intense rainbow arched across the lake, spanning the promontory fort, with the red-orange-yellow sequence beginning on the outside and moving inwards. As the rainbow faded, a cuckoo started calling. It was blustery, too. I pulled over at the foot of Buckoogh and noticed a new fence along the road: the route to Buckoogh would now involve a detour. The first time I climbed it I had just stepped off the road and was away, but since that day some new regulation had waved its dismal wand and ordered barbed wire between the walker and the hill.

The lower road along the lake was closed for resurfacing. The upper road was narrow, with grand old hawthorns heaped with blossom. (Jessica says that no matter how old and gnarled the hawthorn is, its blossom is always young and new.) Hazel and willow were also thick and lush.

The newly surfaced road at Srahmore took me to the river. I parked near the footbridge and went through a gate into the forestry; a stonechat male had made his home in the wreckage of clearfelling and he called to me. His white collar gave him an air of formality in the wilderness.

The forestry road seemed an elaborate fixture for a ritual of felling that takes place only every thirty-five years or so. Newly seeded pines stood like spectators all along the route, and their flowers were like baubles on a Christmas tree. Then I passed a row of four cedars from the time of the original plantation, a decorative gesture by the foresters. And I came across a neat stone channel built with elaborate care, taking a tiny stream down to a culvert running under the track: many years ago, one of the workers made this tribute to water and stone in a quiet week.

The clearfelled areas, in the murk of cloudy spells, looked like a former battlefield being reclaimed by brushy shoots of new pines, with a screen of birch and alder along the road.

If Glennamong was quiet then, it still harboured

memories of the Troubles in Northern Ireland. During the late twentieth century, it was a training ground for the IRA, where volunteers could easily keep a lookout from the top of *Torc Shléibhe* and Ben Gorm. There is an IRA propaganda video from the eighties, where armed men in combat outfits, carrying heavy weapons, are seen moving through forestry plantation on a murky, foggy day. It may well have been filmed here. There are still stories in local memory of IRA men in the area coming into safe houses at night, and of their manoeuvres to outfox the law.

The track that I was following eventually petered out, and I crossed a sheep fence, still within the forest, but the ground was now wet and broken by footprints of sheep and the boot prints of the farmer. I cursed the economy that had planted such a crop of spiky, inert trees in these valleys, and allowed farmers to throw hundreds of sheep on the uplands, merely for the subsidies.

In several places, I noticed instruments of scientific data-gathering: solar panels and rain gauges; troughs had been set into the bed of streams, about ten feet by two, with an aluminium spout to measure water flows. The water was the colour of pale ale, with a beery swirl of froth on top. The scientists could then produce their charts of data showing rainfall amounts, with seasonal variations, as well as rates of run-off. I had heard of other work in this area on the acidification of streams caused by afforestation. It all amounted in my mind to an elaborate autopsy on something that had already succumbed. My beloved salmon and sea trout were being hit at every turn, from the sheep-infested uplands, through the acidic forestry streams, into Newport

Bay with its fish farming. In the middle of it all, state bodies and learned institutions were there to give us exact statistics about the degradation, without any apparent clout to change things.

These angry thoughts were interrupted when I glimpsed an accipiter hawk in the air above the firebreak: brownish, with a flash of bright undertail coverts. It moved off to the left to avoid me, a blue nuisance at the edge of its vision; but then it turned back and reappeared for an instant to check that it got me right first time, turned away again, then came into view one last time, doing a woodpigeon's air-dive, just to show off. And then, nothing more; that was all I saw that day. In the final performance, I got an impression of bulk, saying 'goshawk' instead of 'sparrowhawk', but its appearance was so fleeting that I could not be sure. Instead of a confirmed goshawk, I recorded a *ghosthawk*, one of those rare raptors that linger on the edge of vision, that our imaginations yearn for, that the wet day and the impossible perspectives of the forestry plantation overwhelm.

Since the spread of non-native conifers in the west and south of Ireland, there has been a small dividend of bird species taking advantage of this new habitat, but goshawks are as yet barely a rumour in the west of Ireland. While they have done well in similar habitat in Wales, and there are a few pairs established in the north and south of the country, the chance of seeing a goshawk in the Mayo forests is too remote to warrant a whole day's hunt; it is only a haunting thought.

I followed a stream to get to the upper edge of the plantation, where the spruce trees grow close to each other and create shelter. The forest floor is deeply carpeted with fallen needles, making the ground spongy underfoot and relatively dry: the stream meandering among the tree trunks drains rainwater away. This would be a good pitch for a tent, I thought, under the protective canopy of the trees. I camped out in a situation like this as a lad with trunks of conifers clustered round the light of my campfire. I had left home on a reckless impulse, to travel for a few days during school time like Pádraig Ó Conaire, who caught thrushes in a wood at night and roasted them on a fire, as described in his book *M'Asal Beag Dubh* ('My Little Black Donkey'). My own efforts at self-sufficiency failed on that occasion: I raided a woodpigeon's nest for its white eggs, but I did not venture to eat them, thinking that they might be developed.

When I left the plantation and these boyhood associations, I emerged under a steep, rocky spur running off Glennamong. The rock lies in strata at a forty-five-degree angle, and great slabs are becoming detached, century by century. They lie strewn about the slope above the pine trees, large, flattish boulders from wheelbarrow- to powerboat-size. They are too big – and some too recent – for the bog vegetation to cover them completely, so they offer bare rock to the elements, and bring the wheatear up into these corries. They also form a variety of little grottoes and niches for ferns and flowers. One of them was so big that, as I peered into its depths, I half expected a hermit of the mountain to leer back at me. Bilberry thrives here if it gets enough light, as does opposite-leaved golden saxifrage, while the ferns manage to take shape in permanent shade. And once, between two slabs that had tilted apart to form a trench the size of a large bathtub, I discovered a profusion of wood sorrel and lesser celandine.

The rock was breaking up from the side and formed an even slope on the flank of the mountain: no ledges, no overhangs there. I wanted to take a look around the corner, into the very top of the valley, and this meant an extra hike to a shoulder. The ground was wet, showers were blowing into the corrie all the time, and cloud covered the mountaintop. Twenty minutes farther in I could see the very extremity of the corrie under Glennamong, a cold, grey corner known locally as *Poll Dubh* ('black hole'). One or two ledges might have served for an eyrie, but nothing was showing there that day, no peregrines and no ravens. I walked to within eighty metres of the steepest rocks and scanned the face for suitable ledges, but there was nothing there with the right measure of grandeur. I made this judgement even though my binoculars had fogged up and their assistance was poor.

A new noise was around me: wind running over the bare crags overhead made a sound like the dull roar, almost a growl, when a plane has just landed. I came across a fresh heap of grouse droppings – so fresh that the bird must have been disturbed and flown off before I noticed. The overgrazing was severe, with much of the heather cover gone, so I was surprised to find this bird. At 2 p.m., my preset turnaround time, I started to pick my way back down.

On my right there was a tiny corrie, the smallest I had ever come across, with pond skaters. Jessica suggested that I call it Lough Jacuzzi, which sounded perfect. A small stream ran out of it, one of several that gathered off the mountain to form the Glennamong river, and this I followed down. It directed me back towards the plantation.

This water met some big boulders on its way, and created a series of pools and cascades; beside one tiny cascade, a fresh bouquet of St Patrick's cabbage was just out of reach of grazing sheep, being sprayed continuously by the stream. I entered the plantation, following the stream, and here and there it deepened into dark, peaty stretches along a narrow trench. I found the lolloping track of an otter, a sure sign that there were fish here, trout or eels, the otter's favourite food.

In the middle of the plantation, I crossed a few acres where the trees had not prospered owing to something in the ground conditions. Instead of a dense, shady forest of trees up to twenty-five feet high, these had reached only ten feet and were so meagre-looking that you could walk among them. I imagined myself in a wild taiga in Lapland or Siberia and I had to check to assure myself that these were plantation trees, growing in regular lines.

When I got back to the car I disturbed a common sandpiper from the gravelled road. This bird of upland streams and lakes likes the gravelly banks along the watercourses and here he had found an extra stretch of gravel in the forestry road. I hoped his mate would not decide to lay her eggs in the middle of the thoroughfare.

Corraun Mountains
May 28

Corraun is a peninsula separating Achill Island from the mainland; on the map it appears roughly circular in shape, with an extensive plateau weighted to its southern side, overlooking

Clew Bay. This plateau bears the marks of glaciation as a series of prominent spurs and escarpments. One of Ussher's correspondents, John Le Warden Page, reported 'two or three' eagles' nests in the Corraun mountains, and I had often admired the shoulder extensions off the plateau on its eastern and northern sides as excellent faces for soaring birds.

I approached from Mulranny, and parked on the coast road near Dooghbeg, a famous surfing spot on Clew Bay. A tarred track led up to a transmitter mast at 181 metres, so the first half hour of the walk was easy, steadily rising above bright-yellow gorse bushes. Down at the shore near the pier the council was clearing back boulders thrown up by a famous winter storm in January 2014 that wrecked car parks, promenades and coastlines everywhere. The whine and rattle of two big diggers were loud and clear.

On my first pause to make notes, a green hairstreak butterfly flew around me, interested in my shirt. Butterwort was in flower beside the track. The usual bits of waste metal and rubble were in a few recesses near the road, and old wood cuttings and pallets had been piled on a hearth ready for the St John's Eve bonfire on June 23 – the vantage point was good, overlooking the bay.

As Clew Bay came into view, the drumlin islands reminded me of the Greek fleet at Aulis, waiting for a favourable wind to take it to Troy: there only the faintest pulse of a wave breaking on the shore as a sickle-thin margin. Croagh Patrick, the Sheeffry Hills and Mweelrea were all distinct in outline, on the far side of an immense stretch of sheltered sea. The diggers worked on with their tiny arms, making a pathetic gesture at a rising ocean.

I stopped again on a moraine, with a flat, boggy glen between me and the mountain, which I decided to skirt, taking a drier ridge. This ridge curved around the top of the glen and offered a dry, gradual ascent up to the eastern 'Ben Bulben' brow of the mountain, with its falls and extensive areas of heather. The browner sections of the slope were crossed by stone-coloured lines where sheep had traced their paths.

The rock here is red sandstone, which we have in the stonework of the annexe at our house, and I was surrounded by it as I sat, making notes and eating an apple. On this slope, much of the stone contains quartz pebbles of various sizes, grape-sized, egg-sized, and these have been bonded together – is it by pressure? – so that the rock looks like a conglomerate, or a primitive concrete of rough gravel. A group of these large conglomerate rocks stands clear of the heather, like a dolmen with a capstone.

The heat of the day was beginning to tell, so when I came across a peaty pool I had my first swim of the year outdoors and splashed about for a few minutes, waist deep in water. Praeger was right about the restorative effect of a swim on days like this, and I pushed on, greatly revived.

Instead of trying to skirt the base of the plateau to take a short cut to the other side, I decided to step directly up the flank of the mountain. The rock was broken up into big blocks with even layers, like the edge of an untrimmed book, or an accordion. In places, the layers were breaking apart as flagstones of different shapes and sizes. Climbing here was like stepping up a ruined staircase, taking care not to push through peat and heather into a leg-breaker.

Then, within a few metres, the ground levelled out, and I was onto the Corraun plateau, the strangest ground I had seen so far. The floor is a litter of sandstone, less red than grey because of weathering, with a sparse cover of mat grass, the signature plant of overgrazing. Fifty metres ahead, I saw a cairn the shape of a small wigwam, the stones stacked to a neat point about two metres high, but this was not the highest point: that was marked by another cairn, shaped like a beehive, a couple of hundred metres away to the west, at the true summit (541 m). I discovered others, some just smaller replicas of the big ones, all around this plateau. They looked more like effigies in some ritual space than marks of altitude. And a few horned sheep were loitering around like initiates in a cult. I looked down at my feet to see a cinnabar moth fluttering on the ground. What was it doing up here? I remember them from childhood, when we used to holiday in the dunes at Inch Strand in Kerry.

Running westwards from one of these cairns, an ancient line of stones was set in the ground, marking a boundary between Clew Bay and Blacksod, in some long-forgotten theatre of power, and perhaps of violence, whose players were unknown.

To the north, the interior of the Corraun Peninsula was carpeted with conifers. And on this side of the mountain were the cliffs that I had been searching for. I moved to the right, to get a view of the crags above Lough Cullylea, a ten-metre face formed by stacks of sandstone, but the cliff was meagre, and there were approaches that would make it vulnerable. Over to the west, I glimpsed a darker face just under the summit and decided to trek out across a kilometre of desert to investigate.

My ears were alert to sounds – the skylark was there – but sometimes a squeak from a strap on my rucksack deceived me.

Then a thin sound came repeatedly – the call of the golden plover, a precious summer visitor to these uplands, which has become the symbol of the Ballycroy National Park. I stopped to try to locate the bird, and at first I could only hear it; then, as I was moving closer, coming farther into the territory, the piping got faster, at a higher pitch. Eventually, I saw it seventy metres away, the proud black belly, white margin, and a rich gold mottling on the back. The beak parted briefly each time it called. I searched about to see if I could spot its companion, but could not find another among the rocks.

As the day's excursion was not about breeding golden plovers, I kept going past the bird and paused to watch it moving away in little runs towards where its nest must be. Eventually, dizzy from staring through binoculars at a scrap of mottled gold, I continued towards the horizon, and as the prospect opened up, I said to myself, 'now there is something.'

Just off the summit a series of escarpments formed a wide upper rim to the corrie above Lough Cullydoo. The face was in three main vertical sections, with almost sheer slopes between them, too steep to scramble without climbing equipment. The lower section of cliff was like a fortress above a steep scree fall. The place was almost perfectly designed for an eagle's eyrie. Because the sandstone was structured in blocks and layers with flat sides, in a few places chunks of rock had fallen out of the face, leaving a ledge with a sheltered recess, perfect for a nest. As I searched the cliff with binoculars, I counted at least three sites that looked ideal; the corrie was a theatre haunted by ghosts of eagles past.

The eastern rim, which I stepped down into briefly, was not as forbidding, but when I walked along to a point above the main escarpment and looked back to where I stood, I saw a few more possible ledges. Now the full magnificence of this corrie came home to me: there were in fact two tiers to the coum above Lough Cullydoo. The top tier, which I had been marvelling at, was formed of red sandstone; but there was a lower tier, below the top bowl of scree, formed of the other, older metamorphic rock. And this had its own escarpment, overlooking the lake: there were one or two suitable spots on this face as well. A raven pair flew across the face of the lower tier; for once, I was above them and could see the bluish sheen on their upper plumage.

I thought it remarkable that the map had not prepared me for the best feature: the upper tier of cliffs just below the plateau. It appeared as just a bunching of ten-metre contours between 530 and about 470 metres. The contours merged into a dark shade on the pink elevation.

There were a few other possibilities that I would have to keep for another day's work above Lough Knockacorraun, in another corrie east of Corraun Hill, the last summit in this range at 524 metres. Without a car to collect me on the western side of the peninsula, I had to retrace my steps, with the best find so far at Cullydoo. John Le Warden Page's report of eagle nests on Corraun had become entirely convincing. And, as a final corroboration, there were satellite records of the young golden eagle (Orange 4) from 2006 frequenting the corries on Corraun: 'Once an eagle rock, always an eagle rock.'

On the return, I rose one hare and a grouse near Cushlecka, not far from the transmitter. Either of these was potential prey for an eagle. The wind had risen, so I forwent the chance of a second swim that afternoon. Green hairstreak butterflies were everywhere along the tarred track, boasting their underwings of green neon. It was strange to find them here, so much higher than the gorse, which was their food plant.

Downpatrick Head

June 1

The day's drive was the start of my searches along the north Mayo coast: that breezy, forbidding balcony overlooking Donegal Bay. I presented it to Jessica as a mystery tour that would include a coastal walk, so she was surprised when we headed east, along Beltra Lough, and turned north to Crossmolina. We took the pine marten dashing across the road at Glenisland as a good omen for the day. We had deferred an earlier plan, to walk up Corraun Hill and finish the search of Corraun, because the forecast said a stiff breeze and showers along the coast were expected. The top of Nephin was covered in low cloud and I felt vindicated at having abandoned hillwalking for the day.

Although the outing was devoted to a wild, open space, we gave in to a different impulse as we approached Crossmolina and pulled in at Enniscoe House. Perhaps there is a subtle agoraphobia in us, a fear of having our souls stolen in the immensities of unmarked landscapes, which draws us to the shelter of trees and gardens. The grounds of Enniscoe House offered just such a comfort.

We discovered that the house and gardens were not

scheduled to open until half past one, and we had the woods virtually to ourselves. A walk in broadleaved woodland should, in theory, be a walk into a wild, ancient element of our landscape, but since the ancient woodlands were largely cleared through successive stages of exploitation, deciduous woodland is as deeply marked, culturally and historically, as any landscape type in Ireland.

Nowadays, many tracts of semi-natural woodland are near big houses, a remnant of Romantic style, where the house was set in a picturesque landscape of trees. The lords of the manor held on to their acres of parkland near the house, even after the time came for them to surrender their estates to their erstwhile tenants under reforming Land Acts. These remnants of oak and beech woodland in many instances are now public amenities, with the big houses in the care of the state.

As we walked through the mixed woodland at Enniscoe, the leafy shelter, plus the variety of ground flora, were greatly imbued with my nostalgia for another time, a kind of fin-de-siècle longing. I was pointing out some new bird songs to Jessica, and indicated a thicket where a blackcap was in full voice. The blackcap is a bird that has spread rapidly and extensively throughout the west of Ireland in recent decades, but I still count it as a historical ornament, because in the seventies it made its first summer appearance near my Limerick home at the poet Aubrey de Vere's County Limerick estate, where Tennyson had been a guest.

In an older section of the woods dominated by a few very old beech trees, we heard a loud, rich, vigorous song from a song thrush. We could see the bird clearly, perched on the stump of a rotten side branch that extended horizontally from the trunk of an old beech at a height of twenty feet. This meant that it could see us, and still was undeterred from its performance.

If anyone doubts the individuality of birds and wild creatures generally, they only have to listen to the variations in the thrush's song. The bird at Enniscoe was extremely vigorous and versatile, like a virtuoso that arrived near our house one evening in springtime. This new arrival sang just as it was getting dark, in richer, more exotic tones than our regular song thrush, and it was completely distinct from the bird that had been hammering away through the wet, unsettled weeks after Christmas. I had transcribed the notes of our regular bird as follows:

weed-it, **weed**-it
leave-it, **leave**-it, **leave**-it
do-**wit**, do-**wit**, do-**wit**
widdit, **wid**dit, **wid**dit
tee-**up**, tee-**up**, tee-**up**
gota**b**revit, gota**b**revit, gota**b**revit
will he **ever**, will he **ever**, will he **ever**
to**wid**dit, to**wid**dit, to**wid**dit
do-**wit**, do-**wit**, do-**wit**
churrup, **chur**rup, **chur**rup
chup, chup, chup, chup
gota**cred**it, gota**cred**it, gota**cred**it
will he **ever,** will he **ever,** will he **ever,**

The morning after the newcomer turned up, I got up at 6 a.m. to try to transcribe its notes, but I could hear only a weaker subsong version, with less repetition, from our regular thrush (the other bird must have been passing through on migration, and did not stay):

weet, weet, weet
come-on-in-you-skinny
thin-you
will-he-won't-he
chi-chi
caw-lily
weal, weal
wit, wit, wit
call-a-lily
chivvy-it, **chiv**vy-it
tree-yull
thron, thron, thron
teu-u, teu-u, teu-u
rilly-up-you
weet-u
d'you bit

By transcribing the song of a bird in this way I caught
reverberations from the language I knew; there were scraps
of language here that connected me with the folk element
in English, children's rhymes and colloquialisms, and stray
fragments of meaning whose origins were lost to the memory;
I could not do this in any other language that I have learned.
(Maybe this is what Synge had in mind when he said that the
language of seabirds is easier than the Gaelic, as he watched
them from his seat on Inismaan.) To express the variation in
the song of the thrush, I had to transpose it into my native
language; and I imagine that, for anyone in doubt as to which
is their native language, this exercise would be a litmus test.

As we are constantly attaching our meanings to nature,
I felt surrounded by history in the woods at Enniscoe. The
paths were lined with natives such as tutsan, pignut and
sanicle, but the woods themselves contained admixtures of

spruce and beech, and exotics such as camellia and bamboo. The rich songs of the thrush and blackcap were implicated in an imperial past, as if they were descended from birds that had serenaded gentlemen and ladies in the garden shortly before the First World War. Politics in the woodlands: the seed cases of elm floated around us like ceremonial confetti as we came back to the car.

Leaving Crossmolina, you approach the north Mayo coast along the road to Ballycastle, driving through twenty kilometres of farming country. A change in the landscape comes as a series of hills covered in blanket bog, before you ever get a glimpse of the sea. My imagination was running on the wild coastline west of Ballycastle, but the landlady at the coffee shop in Ballycastle suggested Downpatrick Head, so after lunch we went east to the cliffs and sea stack of *Dún Briste* ('broken fort'). Our hostess showed us a copy of new plans to modernise the visitor experience at Downpatrick Head and replace the rusted fences and scrappy signage. A set of high fences kept us away from a couple of blowholes as we crossed the headland towards the cliffs, and there were many warnings about danger, but the approach to the cliff edge itself was unimpeded: this was once possible at the famous Cliffs of Moher in County Clare, before a series of official developments contrived to wreck the experience.

From the map, Downpatrick Head does not look very promising for the eagle hunter, whose eye is drawn to the higher coastline to the west, but the headland rises to a sheer fifty-metre drop at the end. Air, rock and water are the elements here; and during the summer the cacophony of nesting seabirds is added to the 'modality of the visible'.

Jessica called to me as a peregrine tiercel came off the sea stack and rode the updraught off the cliff. Sea pink was in flower all over the headland, a bouquet from the sea. The turf was shaped into green tussocks about two feet across, feeling spongy underfoot, like a green variant on the basalt forms at Giant's Causeway.

A few anglers came back across the headland to their cars with bags full of gear and fish. Jessica told me that they were speaking Russian. We saw two others spinning for mackerel from the clifftop, like a modern version of the fishing scene from Flaherty's *Man of Aran*. Our Man of Downpatrick was from Putin's Russia and drove a white van. Out on the sea below him, an inflatable rib with a fully suited crew was being driven through the water with the power of an SUV. It slowed down and drifted slowly on the rocking surface near the sea stack with its white-stained ledges and choirs of guillemots and kittiwakes. The sea was busy with more of these birds in loose flotillas, and fulmars soaring back and forth, but, in the absence of the sea eagle, the sovereign here was the gannet. Two or three were turning at height a kilometre away, patrolling the waters for fish. They were in mature plumage, so they may have been breeding birds, which had come all the way from a colony in Kerry to join the Russian anglers at these rich waters.

Because of the geology of this coast, the rock has formed deep recesses and wide ledges for the birds. In a few places the guillemots were four deep on the ledge; sea eagles could have made a home here in the days of abundance. One ledge in particular, fairly high up, was deep and sheltered by an extending layer overhead; its only disadvantage was that the cliffmen could have secured a rope on the top and lowered a man down a few metres to within reach of the nest. I decided that, the day sea eagles came to nest here, I would have to join forces with the state and ban visitors from the clifftop.

This scene at Downpatrick Head is set against the backdrop of steep coastline to the west. A foreshortening effect of perspective, similar to that at the Cliffs of Moher, causes the cliffs at Céide, the point at Benwee Geevraun, and the sharp peak of Glinsk seventeen kilometres away to be bunched together and form one sublime and forbidding cluster, with cliffs much higher than those at Downpatrick Head. On the day of our visit the outlines were darkened by overcast conditions, so there was an ominous effect in the air to add to the forbidding profile of the coast. I was not the first to be impressed. After his first visit to the area with a friend in June 1898, Ussher wrote in his journal, 'The grandeur and picturesqueness of this coast far exceed that of any other that Howard Sanders and I have seen.' About sixty years earlier, Canon Otway had travelled this coast by boat, and later wrote, 'Certainly of all the sea scenery I had ever witnessed, what I now enjoyed was incomparably the most varied and most grand.'[17]

Part of its appeal is its remoteness and inaccessibility, then as now. The modern road past Céide and Belderg turns inland towards Glenamoy and retreats from those wild headlands. There is, however, an inner road that runs closer to the coast and takes you to Porturlin and Portacloy. As you approach Belderg, you see the first stretch climbing the hillside above the village; notionally, you are now in the Gaeltacht, but to hear Irish as a living speech, you have to go farther west to

Portacloy and the Carrowteige district. This is one of the last enclaves of the language in Mayo, and it corresponds to the sea eagle's historical heartland. The journey there takes you through the townlands of Glinsk, Laghtmurragha and Srahataggle, which slope upwards towards the sheer precipices above the sea.

But that would be a journey for another day. On this occasion we kept to the main road towards Glenamoy and drove home. Later that evening I marked the north Mayo eagle sites in ink on the OS Discovery map (sheet 23), and showed them to Jessica. My trawl through the historical records had come up with at least eight sea-eagle locations along this northern rim of the county.

Corraun Hill
June 3

A bog track from the village allowed me to drive up the slope for the first kilometre or so. When I got to the end there was another car parked near turf workings where a man was gathering sods into plastic bags. I parked and set out on foot.

A grey zone of showers was crossing Clew Bay south of Clare Island. Clare Island itself was in sunlight, with a good view of the steep slopes and cliffs at the back of Knockmore. With the sun in the south, part of this face was in shadow; one high, rectangular recess looked like a huge cave. On either side of this recess, there were vertical faces and folds where golden eagles bred, according to Ussher, up to 1878.

The species became a target here, as elsewhere in Mayo, in the name of preserving grouse stocks. The last bird was killed in 1887 and is preserved in the Natural History Museum.

When Praeger arrived on his first visit to Clare Island in 1902 he spent much of his time scrambling across the northern ledges and slopes of this forbidding coastal mountain, where he found a range of arctic-alpine plants that excited him so much that he set off on a scientific journey to explore the history of Irish vegetation. His first article on the botany of Clare Island contains the following boast about his fieldwork on this fearsome precipice:

> This great cliff falling into the sea is inconvenient to examine, because of the shattered and crumbling nature of the slates of which it is composed; but by dint of patience I explored it from the summit to within reach of the waves, in spite of heavy rain, and accompanying difficulties of foothold.[18]

The plants he found here threw up all sorts of questions about species that had survived the last Ice Age and, more generally, about the origins of the Irish flora. Clare Island became the focus of Praeger's fascination with island biogeography, and he eventually persuaded the Royal Irish Academy to fund a series of scientific expeditions here between 1909 and 1911. Under his direction, teams of specialists in every biological field combed the island and surrounding sea for three seasons, to record as many plant and animal species as possible. The final species list in the three large tomes of results published by the Academy ran to 8,488, of which 398 were new to the British Isles and 120 new to science. The survey was a masterpiece of Victorian 'faunistics', or species inventories. It was also a poignant marker of a world of innocent privilege that was about to be smashed open by the horrors of the First World War and the Troubles in Ireland. There is a photograph from 1910 of a group of visiting scientists posing in a traditional boat, a *pucaun*, on the beach at Clare Island. The bonhomie has been muted for a moment by the photographer: Praeger himself is caught in half profile in a distinct white jacket, seated at the back, with his signature mariner's gaze into the distance. The photographer and conchologist Robert Welch balances Praeger's posture at the opposite end of the row: he, too, is staring out to sea. The rest look absent-minded; no one is smiling in a self-promotional way, because no one's career depended on the image in those years.

In one important respect, the Clare Island Survey failed: Praeger's original prospectus gave as one of the aims of the fieldwork to compare the island's flora and fauna with that of the mainland, to examine 'variation produced by isolation'; he was clearly dreaming about the island as a kind of Irish Galapagos, where isolation had produced endemic forms: those famous markers of evolution studied by Darwin. None of the results bore out this hope. The island had only recently separated from the mainland after the last glaciation about 10,000 years ago; this was far too little time, in evolutionary terms, for endemic life forms to develop.[19]

As I climbed the hill I watched a procession of light showers along the southern half of the bay, and I texted weather reports to Jessica and her colleagues who were cycling from Newport to Mulranny. The showers moving in their direction were light, and there was brightness behind them, I reported, from my weather station on the hill.

Salmon cages were visible at Clare Island harbour, and there were others, fine black rings on the water a few kilometres out. Occasionally, a boat scored the sea with a white puff of spray. The sea was blue in the sun, and the tongues of land stretching into the water at Corraun were vividly green. The moorland slope below me was marked with a fine pattern of cuttings on the dark green – old peat workings, now mostly abandoned, except for one man bent over his bright bags of turf. I came across grouse droppings at about 400 metres, not fresh but the only sign of this bird I saw all morning.

I came up onto the shoulder at 450 metres with Achill spread out in front of me. The oyster beds at Corraun were dark, geometric rows in the shallow inlet running up to Achill Sound. A suburbia of houses clustered along the shore. I turned away and continued up the hill.

The last section of the climb was the most interesting. The ground got stonier, more exposed, the heather reduced to a low, tight mass with an admixture of golden moss. Bell heather was there in a tiny bonsai version, with a red-tipped lichen on the same scale. I was admiring tormentil and fresh bilberry leaves when, to my delight, I discovered mats of sea pink among the stones; the blossoms were shivering on their stalks, and I thought of this mountain slope, at nearly 500 metres, as an extension of the breezy headlands along the sea. The salt breezes get fetched up here, and a few stray seeds had come with them.

I sat down in this rock garden to make notes. Each rock was so rich in mica that they glinted in the sun like aluminium foil. The golden moss was the colour of my jacket lining. And here and there, among the bilberry and sea pink, were red stalks of St Patrick's cabbage.

Out on top of the plateau, I was away from the breeze shaking the stems of the thrift. Bilberry was around me in profusion, recovering, as was fir clubmoss, like miniature pine trees. I sat in the lee of the lower summit, overlooking Lough Knockacorraun, with a skylark over me, at about 600 metres.

There are five shoulders off the north side of Corraun mountain, with great scree falls, escarpments and some areas fully denuded of vegetation. Two corries west of the impressive bowl of Cullydoo, there is another wide escarpment of red sandstone near the top of the corrie, though it is not as steep or pronounced.

I set out to get a view of the slopes underneath me, and headed east, following the rim of the corrie. No sooner had I heard the first call of a golden plover than I rose a pair, which flew off towards the wetter, boggy ground of the saddle at about 420 metres. I was drawn to the edge of the corrie, where the slope falls suddenly, steeply towards the lake 160 metres farther down. This is the kind of ground where you can easily get caught out, as a slope gets steeper, and within a short distance you find yourself scrambling on an unstable slope, with a vertical face beneath you, and nothing to break your fall. I stepped down to the very top of the rim to get the best gallery seat and leant back carefully, making sure not to get tangled in the straps of my binoculars or rucksack. Corraun Hill was over to my left, and I could see the cliff under the summit, with boulder scree beneath it running towards the lake at the bottom. This crag has a sheer, vertical overhang, with a longer, broader apron of rock under it; right at the top of the apron there are one or two boulders lodged upright, with a space behind, where a nest could be supported. An eyrie in this position would be completely inaccessible to anyone without climbing gear.

Wind was tugging at the hood of my jacket, and its rushes and surges dominated the soundscape; I also heard the sound of water from small streams draining the mountain. Wind in the bowl of the corrie pushed this watery sound upwards, filling the air. The calls of a few birds added their tiny embroidery to the rushing wind-water backdrop: meadow pipit, wren and wheatear. Lough Knockacorraun is a lopsided oval with a sickle-shaped raft of brown *Potamogeton* leaves close to its southern shore where this species of water plant manages to prosper. A stream off the mountain had created a small, sandy delta at the lake with grassy pasture around it where sandy deposits had improved the drainage. A breeze had got up across the lake; it skidded briefly on the surface at first and made a few fairy-like appearances and vanishings, then it applied itself more thoroughly. Through the binoculars I watched the scale-like pattern of the surface waves moving in one direction from right to left; the shapes had the consistency of a design on bright, beaten metal. The binoculars isolated the image, extracted it from the scene, and made it abstract; I imagined these recorded on video and placed in one of the temples of contemporary art.

Then it was time to go. I got up carefully and stepped clear of the steep drop. As I crossed the saddle back towards the south, the view shifted within a few paces towards Clew Bay. On this flatter ground in the lee of Corraun Hill, the bog had accumulated into a wet moor with flushes where my plover pair had made their home, and their calls were around me as I passed. A grey wall of rain was moving into the bay from the south-west, so I quickened my pace through the heather to avoid a wetting and made it back to the car as the first drops speckled my jacket.

Slievemore
June 8

Jessica and I drove to Achill to call on Francis van Maele and Antic-Ham at the Red Fox Press in Doogort, on the northern side of the island. Francis and Ham, who go by the dual name Franticham, have established their art-book press in a renovated cottage and outhouse overlooking Blacksod Bay. The setting is majestic, if a little terrifying, on a low cliff overlooking Doogort Strand, with Slievemore to the left, and the great expanse of Blacksod Bay straight ahead. Franticham spend much of their time travelling to art-book fairs in North America and Europe, so it felt like our good fortune to find them at home. We stepped into the crowded space of their cottage kitchen, past a sign saying 'Sorry, We're Open', and when our eyes adjusted to the gentle shade of the interior, their art books and prints were spread on tables and filling shelves.

Francis's typography designs reference Dada and Fluxus, those scrapbook styles that are the hallmark of modernism in middle Europe. He and Ham are also great enthusiasts of Polaroid photography, and their books gather together a rich – even obsessive – record of their travels from Seoul to California. We linger over Ham's prints: almost every day she draws and colours a cartoon-style scene from their ordinary encounters and posts it on Facebook. Many of them are reproduced as separate prints, and she also collects the best of these in little album books. I bought one of the Achill albums for the library at home.

As we were getting into our Fiat 500, Ham followed us out to take a Polaroid snap, and it delighted – if it did not surprise – us to see her drawing of me and Jessica beside the sky-blue Fiat, on her Facebook page a few days later.

The evangelist Edward Nangle founded a Protestant mission at Doogort in 1831 and led a campaign of religious and social reform with missionary zeal here for many years. The remnants of his failed empire give a settled character to the village. There is an appealing gloom under the thick foliage of sycamores, willows and fuchsias in the groves around the old assembly hall; calla lilies, that staple of west-of-Ireland cottage gardens, flower here profusely. Nangle's legacy extends beyond Doogort to the now defunct chapel on Inisbiggle nearby, where a small Protestant community subsisted for many years until the late twentieth century. A later visitor to Doogort was the German author Heinrich Böll, whose house at the other end of the settlement is now run as an artists' and writers' retreat by the Heinrich Böll Foundation.

As my thoughts were turning on the old eyrie site at Slievemore, we abandoned our historical sightseeing to go for a walk on the beach. The mountain was partly in cloud, so we could not get a satisfactory view of the cliff that held eagles up to the early nineteenth century. Nonetheless, it was easy to identify the site described by W. H. Maxwell: 'a huge and inaccessible crag on the east side of Slievemore, and immediately above the coastguard station'.

Maxwell's account of sea eagles at Doogort comes from his compendium of anecdotes about Mayo, published in 1832 as *Wild Sports of the West of Ireland*. The author was a hunter, adventurer and raconteur whose turbulent career in the Anglican Church eventually brought him to Balla (pronounced 'baal') near Castlebar. Along with this office, Maxwell got the livings of three parishes in the county, which allowed him to spend his time carousing with the soldiery in Castlebar, collecting tales of military life, and indulging his passion for outdoor adventure in west Mayo. He thrived so much in military company that Maxwell later drew on his Castlebar experiences to publish *Stories of Waterloo* (1829), *Victories of the British Armies* (1839), and a three-volume biography of the Duke of Wellington (1839–41). His adventures in west Mayo were helped by the Marquess of Sligo of Westport House, who gave Maxwell the use of Croy Lodge, at the mouth of the Owenduff river.

When Maxwell came to Doogort in the 1820s, the sea eagle eyrie had been in active use for many years, and the eagles were familiar to the villagers:

Many attempts are made annually to destroy this predatory family; but it is impossible to rob the nest. Situated two hundred feet above the base of the rock, it is of course unapproachable from below, and as the cliffs beetle over it frightfully, to assail it from above would be a hazardous essay. An enterprising peasant, some years since, was let down by a rope and basket, but he was fiercely attacked by the old birds and the basket nearly overturned. Fortunately the cord was strong and had sufficient length to allow his being lowered rapidly, or he would have undoubtedly sustained some bodily injury from the wings and talons of those enraged and savage birds.

Maxwell's account also gives valuable details about the eagles' diet, and supports the contention that sea eagles are no threat to lamb stocks:

On reaching the bottom of the rock, in whose face the eyrie stands, we discovered that the old birds were absent, and, as the nest was formed in a deep fissure, we could not ascertain its situation exactly. But that the eagles' dwelling was above us was evident enough; the base of the cliff was strewn with bones and feathers, and the accumulation of both was extraordinary. The bones of rabbits, hares, and domestic fowls, were most numerous, but those of smaller game, and various sorts of fish, were visible among the heap.[20]

The main nuisance of eagles in those days was the birds' preference for poultry, especially hens with dark plumage, 'to the sad annoyance of the islanders'. Maxwell even contends that the villagers of Doogort 'avoid as much as possible rearing birds of that colour'.

Our excursion ended with a cursory stroll along the road past the old coastguard station, from where Maxwell watched sea eagles with the aid of the coastguards' telescope. We came across Doogort's smart new sewage treatment plant near the roadside; it seemed a humble gesture to the great fetch of sea and shore spread out in front of us, but it acknowledged that even here we should behave respectfully. The eye strained towards vague shapes on the distant sea: the Mullet, Inishkea South, Duvillaun (famous for 'agles and say birds'), and tried to assemble them into a locale; but the dizzying gulf of water, air and distance was too much; it collapsed any arrangement of land around this vast, amorphous bay, and returned us to our compact car and narrow certainties.

Corslieve and Slieve Carr
June 11

Corslieve (721 m) is the highest peak in the Nephin Beg range, a concave sweep of peaks and ridges running for thirty kilometres from Mulranny in the south-west to Bangor Erris in the north. I normally see it on my way to fish for salmon and sea trout on the Owenduff river to the west of the range. From that perspective Corslieve appears as a distant ridge with an ancient cairn, similar to Queen Maeve's cairn on Knocknarea in Sligo. One of the traditional giants of Erris, *Dáithí Bán* ('White David'), is said to have lived here, on the mountain summit.

I met Fergal O'Dowd in Newport before we set out on a walk to the top. Fergal is a former lecturing colleague of mine who combines an adventurer's thirst for Mayo's wild places with a teacher's curiosity about the environment and Gaelic tradition. He suggested that Corslieve is the remotest mountain in Ireland, which is not quite the case if you know the approach from the east along a forestry track. This took us to the base of the mountain near Scardaun, a saddle between Corslieve and Nephin Beg, the next peak to the south. The area has recently been designated the Nephin Wilderness Area, with a few bothies and extra facilities for walkers. We passed an area of recent felling on the way in, where a section of plantation was being cleared to restore a pristine habitat. Most of this area is still densely covered by commercial forestry plantations of lodgepole pine and sitka spruce; a vast tract of plantation opened up to our view as we looked north towards the wind farm at Bellacorick, with the locháns of the old 'flow' moorland glinting here and there in a few unplanted areas.

A new timber staircase took us from the road to a gap in the forestry, and then we slogged our way up the slope, with siskins calling in the trees behind us. As we got to the level of the Scardaun lakes, Fergal rose a grouse, the only one we would see that day. There were encouraging signs of recovery of heather on the southern side of Corslieve, which is within the Ballycroy National Park, and there were some stands of deep growth for nesting grouse. Before attacking the main slope, we went down to the lake at *Coire na Binne* and watched its inert surface for a while. Two rowan trees, one of them especially fresh-looking with new flowers, graced the western shore. The modest-looking crag above *Coire na Binne* has a nice recessed ledge with an overhang, and I added it to the archive. A golden plover called from the saddle of Scardaun as we turned to climb.

I had been given names for the corries at the back of Corslieve so I started counting them in sequence from south to north: *Coire na Binne* ('corrie at the peak'), *Coire na nGarú* ('wild' or 'rough corrie'?), *Coire Tirim* ('dry corrie'), *Coire Leachta* ('corrie [at] the cairn'), *Coire Glas* ('green corrie'). They were all formed during the last Ice Age by a process that writer and cartographer Tim Robinson has described in his *Connemara* trilogy, where 'snow, piling up on the shadowed lea-side of the mountain peaks, congealed into glaciers'.[21]

The scree slope above Scardaun took us quickly to the top of the plateau, and we moved among those strange peat hags with strips of turf that I saw on the way up Birreencorragh in May. As on Birreencorragh, some of the stretches of peat were completely denuded of vegetation and were fringed with fragments of stone: this produced a combination of brilliant white quartz and grey metamorphic rock set in a dark background of peat. Elsewhere, the peat looked as though it had expanded out of the ground like a gradual lava flow, having pushed open the grassy surface.

We reached the top of Coire na nGarú, the finest corrie of all, second in the sequence after Coire na Binne. It had many sections of sheer rock, in two main series, with a virtually inaccessible grassy slope between them. As we were looking and exploring, I heard a familiar call, and a peregrine arrived on rapid, urgent wingbeats from the west, alerted by the unaccustomed sight of two walkers on the ridge above her home. She wheeled out over the vast amphitheatre of the coum, calling repeatedly, and maintained her height with vigorous strokes of broad, powerful wings. There is nothing in the bird world to combine speed and power quite like the peregrine. The bird's silhouette against the grey sky was like a symbol, a form full of ancient wonder and implication, and it perfectly illustrated Yeats's belief in the potency of traditional forms.

Eventually, the shrill, grating call echoing off the cliff walls became oppressive, and we moved on, allowing it to fade out behind us.

Having come so far, to the high point at 572 metres, we

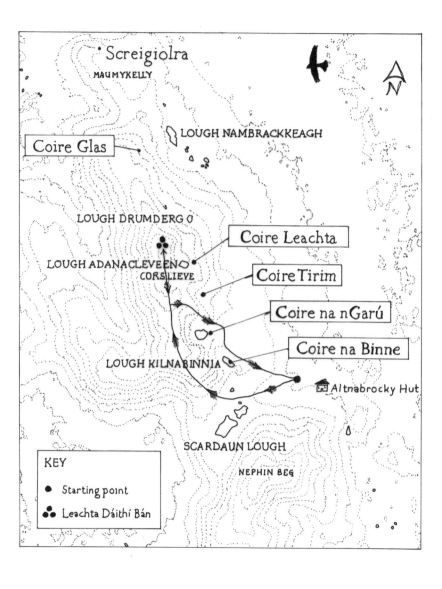

decided to push on to the top of Corslieve, about a kilometre away. Fir clubmoss was growing at our feet, in some places just a yellowish straggler on the bare stones. Cloud blew in from the west, reducing visibility, so I cautiously marked our passage with blocks of quartz in a few places, in case we might have to creep back through fog.

As perspectives opened up again, we could see the ancient cairn and the trig point at the summit of Corslieve emerging from the mist. The cairn of stones, *Leachta Dháithí Bán*, appeared like a fort. It is easy to see how it could have been figured by folklore as a giant's fortress, a heap of loose, angular blocks of rock, the smallest shoe size, the largest just as much as a strong man could lift; and I wonder at the ritual impulse that brought people in ancient times to such a remote place to gather rocks at the top of a mountain. Dáithí Bán must have had his first incarnation here, in a pre-Celtic language, as the tutelary spirit of the place, and got his colour from the blocks of quartz that originally littered the slopes. There are none on the summit now, they must have all been picked up and transported away as sacred trophies, forerunners of the fairy stones of our folklore. Paud McHugh at Tarsaghaun has a large quartz rock set upright at the roadside near his cottage, as if marking the spot where, years ago, his father Paddy first told me about the giant. Elsewhere, throughout the county, people have gathered quartz stones to decorate walls, gateposts and Marian shrines. The ritual impulse with this white stone is diverse and enduring.

Lough Adanacleveen in the bowl of Coire Leachta is set tight under this summit, about 160 metres lower down, glittering even under cloud cover. I said to Fergal I did not think there were any fish there, it being hard to imagine any creature subsisting in its cold, inert waters. Coire Leachta under us was the fourth corrie in the series, starting from Coire na Binne; on the way back we skirted the third, Coire Tirim ('dry corrie'), the only one that does not have a lake at the bottom. For part of the descent, we followed a broad, gradually sloping avenue of smaller loose stones, between which water ran along in a soft glitter. The stones supported our boots, so there was no splashing as we went, though we were walking on water.

A long, snaking ridge led down between Coire Tirim and Coire na nGarú. The peregrine rose again as we descended, with the great coum wall rising to our right. Behind the commotion of this calling falcon, I heard a lower, growling or hissing call, and a search with binoculars found a second bird, presumably the male, moving across the face of the corrie to alight on a rocky slope. I searched the rocky faces for the ghost of an eyrie: one of Ussher's informants, a cliffman from the north Mayo coast, described 'black eagles' he saw coming down from the mountains near Bangor where he supposed them to breed. These are the best cliffs on Corslieve, but there was only one ledge that looked suitable to my landlocked eyes, despite the magnificence of the setting.

As we moved along the ridge, leaving Coire na nGarú, two lesser black-backed gulls appeared from the east, gliding effortlessly on an updraught out of the coum; without moving their wings, their heads turned from side to side as they inspected the ground for carrion; then the wind came down at them from above, making them work their wings for lift. They rose towards the peregrine cliffs, swept across the face of the coum for a few moments, then tilted away again to the east, continuing their patrol of these eastern slopes and hollows where a sheep or a lamb might have died.

My knees and legs were feeling the pressure on the final stretch, as Fergal strolled on ahead of me, apparently immune to the terrain. I made progress by staggering and jolting along, like the young Seamus Heaney in the wake of his father with the plough. As we approached the forestry plantation, and the track where the car was parked, I studied a low crag at Coire na Binne from a new angle and notice a recessed ledge with an overhang set in the vertical face, but it looked as though you could creep up to it on your hands and knees.

Of all the mountains in this range, the eponymous Nephin Beg was the one I felt least inclined to explore. From the Scardaun side, its northern slopes looked dull and degraded, the map offered little prospect of interesting cliffs and outcrops, and the only lakes near it were two on the saddle at Scardaun between it and Corslieve. As we drove out, following the forestry track, a modest hill at 311 metres, Correenbeg, with a fine crag on its north-eastern face, looked more dramatic than anything Nephin Beg had to offer. I passed that dour massif without regret or longing.

It would be many months before I walked to the top of Nephin Beg and made amends for my mean-minded attitude. Although undramatic in itself, ascending it justified Nan Shepherd's view that 'it is worth ascending unexciting heights if for nothing else than to see the big ones from near their own level.'[22] The view of Corslieve from the top of Nephin Beg underlines Corslieve as a fortress with its own lonely eminence rising away from the bulwark of a western ridge at *Tamhnach na Sifín*, ('the mountain field of the bulrushes'). While Corslieve, seen from the distant roads to the west or east, is a ridge of gradual, gentle contours, its dramatic east-facing brow emerges clearly and exclusively when seen from the elevation of Nephin Beg.

Before I made that discovery, my thoughts were running instead on a ridge and a sharp summit south-west of Glennamong, with a corrie to the north called Coire na Binne (another 'corrie at the peak'). The summit itself was unnamed on the OS map and marked only by the symbol for a trig point, along with the elevation. So, in the absence of any place name to locate it, pending further research, I used the altitude mark to give it an abstract title: K716.

Glendahurk
June 12

Glendahurk is the second in a series of four glens embraced by mountain ridges between Newport and Mulranny on the northern rim of Clew Bay. Like Glennamong, the first in the series, its floor has been planted with a dark tongue of conifers. The backdrop to Glendahurk is the most rugged and impressive ridge – technically an arête – formed by the friction between two glaciers, one moving south towards Clew Bay, the other grinding its way north.

My first trip there was an afternoon stroll with Jessica to take a tentative look at what would be in store two days later, when I joined Fergal for a climb of the ridge. We parked near the Owengarve river and walked out across the bog on a waymarked track. I spoke to a turfcutter as he passed in a vehicle and asked him if he had a name for K716, which I pointed to. He was unsure, but thought it might be Nephin Beg; I corrected him politely and continued on. A moment later we flushed a young hare from old cutaway and watched it lope away across the bog. The slopes and ridges of this open country are similar to the landscape on the Isle of Skye where, in 1985, I saw my first golden eagles hunting for rabbits on a low ridge near a corrie lake.

I scanned the cliffs and rocks under the mountain at the top of Glendahurk with binoculars and was daunted at the challenge of having to get my weary legs up there in two days' time, following Fergal's drifting, easy stride.

The bog roads around Glendahurk are neatly marked with colour-coded posts for different circuits and polite signs asking you to close gates. The route we chose took us farther into the wooded glen of Glendahurk. I could hear machinery ahead and wanted to ask someone again if there was a name for the mountain at the top of the valley.

I met two local men of impressive stature at work close to the plantation; when I introduced myself and blustered about an article I had written on eagles, they gave me the information I needed. *Coscéim*, they said, was the local name for the highest point; and one of them added *carra*, which made perfect sense: *an coscéim carrach*, 'the rocky step'. The name actually refers to the narrow ridge from the south-west leading up to K716 itself, and which, they added, was 'only a yard wide'. And they had seen an eagle here, 'about three or four years ago'; their neighbour saw it also, and noticed a wing tag: this was presumably the juvenile sea eagle from Kerry that frequented the area in 2011 and 2012.

They said they were uncertain about some names, because their commonage did not extend into those mountains, but they named the western extension of the arête, a secondary peak at 681 metres, as *Fiddaunmore*. I queried 'fiddaun' as a word meaning 'stream', and they explained that there was a stream coming off the cliffs here, the source of the Owengarve river. They named the summit to our right, the eastern high point, as 'O-hilly', which the OS map marks as Oghillees. When I first spotted this, I fancied that there might be a trace of the great Greek warrior here on a hillside overlooking Clew Bay, but in fact the name comes from *eochaillí* in Irish (meaning 'yew woods').[23] They also said that the Owengarve was 'destroyed' as a river for fishing after the forestry came, and they were worried about the new regulations telling them what they could and could not do on their land. They pointed out with pride that they had never sold land to the forestry, which is why Glenthomas, to the west, was unspoilt to this day.

The information these men gave me showed how volatile place names can be in remote parts of Mayo, where names have been set adrift topographically, with the extinction of the Irish language. Names such as Fiddaunmore, which refer to a feature lower down in the valley, easily get promoted to become the name of the mountain summit overhead. Corrie names such as Coire na Binne ('corrie at the peak') and Coire an Earraigh ('spring corrie'), have a tendency to be applied to the peak itself. K716 was named in a recent map for hillwalkers as either Corr na Binne or Poll Dubh ('black hole'). It is inevitable that the local sheepmen, whose business rarely takes them to the top of these bleak summits, would economise in this way, and use features of more familiar slopes to distinguish the mountaintops.

Glendahurk (*Gleann dá Thorc*) is itself intriguing. *Torc* in Irish has a core meaning of (wild) 'boar', but by extension it can refer to a shaggy heap; in another sense it can mean 'eminent person'. The reference to a boar suggests a mythical influence; the destructive beast is a bearer of power and fertility, and has fascinated poets and mythographers such as W. B. Yeats, Robert Graves, and Ted Hughes. In Irish legend, the boar killed the hero Diarmaid, whose nomadic romance with the heroine Gráinne is marked in a place name at a promontory fort on Lough Feeagh, south of Glennamong. With such a weight of interest attaching to this mythical creature, the boar's influence bears down on Glendahurk, even in the absence of any narrative that I am aware of. In any case, I am satisfied that the two summits at either end of the arête at Coscéim are the two eminences, *dá thorc*. But as *torc* can also refer to an eminent person, I think of the pride of the two big men in Glendahurk who shared their knowledge with me, and I gather their forms along with mythical boars, shaggy heaps and summits, into the shelter of the name.

Coscéim Carrach
June 16

The light woke me soon after 6 a.m. When I came downstairs, the sun was already well up in the sky and crows were moving around the newly mown silage fields, like generals preparing for a battle. Each of the grassblade tips on the lawn carried its own bead of dew. My son Seamus rang two evenings ago, proposing to meet up in Galway. He tells me that little Daniel, who will be six in August, is excited about plans to go to Mountshannon in July to see the Lough Derg sea eagles. He has also promised me one of his drawings, based on a photo of a sea eagle from Mountshannon. I already have two of his drawings on my wall, one of a merlin, and another of a group of three greenshanks, done in detailed, meticulous pencil.

Although Fergal and I had started our walk by 9 a.m., other walkers were ahead of us; we could hear them whooping and calling as they moved up the long ridge between Glenthomas and Glendahurk. Much of the plantation in Glendahurk had been clearfelled and replanted. Glenthomas to the left has no forestry, but there were too many sheep scattered across the valley, more than current designations should allow; Fergal and I talked about the difficulty of getting management plans to work on these commonages when there were so many shareholders. A stiff breeze from the north-east was nagging at us on the exposed part of the ridge, so we walked for a time on the sheltered side overlooking Glenthomas.

The other walkers were high on the ridge ahead of us, still calling and whooping, when we found a smart outdoor ladies' jacket that one of them had just dropped. Conditions were clear, with a view south to Mweelrea and the tip of Connemara at Cleggan, the poet Richard Murphy's country; we eagerly climbed to the top of the ridge to get a view to the north: a vast, flat tract of moorland containing the Owenduff and Bellaveeny catchments. This was the view that dismayed the antiquary Richard Pococke when he crossed the Nephin Beg mountains on August 5, 1752, the first tourist to do so. His journal describes it as 'a morass extending to the sea... The most dismal looking country I ever saw... the greater part irreclaimable.'[24] Pococke crossed the mountains along the Bangor Trail farther east and was put off by the uninterrupted perspectives of Erris. He was more at home among the 'very Romantick' appearances of high mountains and corries. Pococke might have preferred our vantage point: Corranabinna and its shallow lake, shaped like a mirror image of the island of Britain, were at our feet, and beyond that we saw the next corrie and another lake to the east, Corryloughaphuill. The Owenduff was visible, wandering and twisting across the bog on its way to Blacksod Bay, and I pointed out the Blue Lodge of the Rock House fishery, like a blue punctuation dash beside a sandy arc of the riverbank. We agreed that it was 'the best view in Mayo', and the best stretch of wilderness in the country, free of roads and houses, with a scattering of locháns across the blanket bog like small blue fragments of fallen sky. Fergal's eye picked out the islands in Blacksod Bay, where he has travelled by kayak: Inishkea north and south, Duvillaun, Inishglora. He also located the lighthouse at Black Rock, to the north of Achill.

Looking directly north, we could see the headlands of the Mayo coast, as well as Ben Bulben in Sligo, and the farthest, hazy outline of Donegal, from where the eagle eye can easily make out the Mayo coast and the Nephin Beg mountains.

The other walkers were sitting on a tent groundsheet nearby to have their lunch, and we went over to them to deliver the jacket. They were a mixed group of students, full of youthful stamina and exuberance, on a six-week trek along the Atlantic seaboard, from Cork northwards, and their intention was to camp in Mulranny that evening. The jacket owner was astonished that 'Superman' (her word) should appear on the top of the mountain, bearing the garment she realised she had lost. We ate our sandwiches, said farewell, and then continued on towards the arête.

At first sight, the narrow passage across exposed rocks, with a sheer drop on either side into the coums below, seemed almost impossible, but we knew that other hikers had crossed it with fully laden packs on their way to Bangor. Fergal went ahead, and I followed, fixing my hands carefully on the ridges of rocks before putting my weight on them and swinging down. I was careful not to look to either side, only ahead, and I tried to avoid that tightening in the chest that is the onset of fear and defeat. I knew that I was close to ledges and gaps in the rocks where eagles might have settled. The strata had been tilted by ancient movements of the earth to lie vertically, and the rock had broken into great slabs, fins and blocks along this ridge. At one point in the crossing, where there was only one possible step, my boots alighted on a thin, upright blade of rock, like a peg to take me along the face, and I saw that it was worn at this point from the passage of other climbers. Perhaps this very edge of rock was the *coscéim carrach* that gave the entire summit its name.

Then Fergal announced that we were past the most difficult section; the rest of the arête was a steep grassy slope coming up to a vertical drop into Corranabinna, the corrie that gave K716 its borrowed name. The top of this slope was surprisingly thickly carpeted with mat grass and mosses, and there were even a few twitching meadow pipits flitting about on the stone tops. Right at the rim, great wood-rush (*Luzula sylvatica*) grew in profusion, a plant used by golden eagles in Scotland to line their nests.

I believe I would not have attempted Coscéim Carrach on my own, without Fergal's untroubled sense of challenge and curiosity. I looked back across the arête to see one of the young ramblers sitting on a rock near the top, in a pose reminiscent of Caspar David Friedrich's *Wanderer over a Sea of Fog*. Down in Glendahurk, the upper stretch of forestry was shaped like a lady's skirt, the lower slopes formed her torso and arms depicting a dance movement.

When we got to the trig point at K716, several beetles were crawling across the concrete bollard, including two playing piggy-back, like a vehicle tow truck. They, like the bluebottle buzzing around some fresh sheep dung, seemed perfectly at home in this exposed location.

My science had slackened; on my way back down, along the eastern side of Glendahurk, I stopped to survey the lower cliffs and crags at the head of the glen, and I decided that, apart from the cliffs under Coscéim, there was at least one possible eyrie site lower down, below the arête, where a vertical chunk of rock had collapsed out of the strata, like a bread slice missing from a sliced pan. I also noticed two promising ledges at the back, high above the lake in Corranabinna, and there were some other crags on the north-facing side of a coum farther back towards Mulranny, which would have to wait for another day. Fergal went ahead of me to take in an extra summit, *Cnoc Scealpach* ('splintered hill'), above the eastern ridge.

As I came down a steep heathery slope towards the forestry in Glendahurk, a dark shape crossed the sun above me and I thought it might be a raven or a bird of prey moving across the glen. Holding up my cap to shield the sun's intensity, I watched for a bird flying across the glaring sky, but saw nothing. Then, high up, the glitter of a dragonfly appeared, about the size of a transatlantic jet at cruising altitude. It glistened for a moment as it sank and then disappeared; without the high angle of light on its wings, it became a speck too small to see; but for an instant, as it crossed the sun, the shadow at my feet could have been an eagle's.

The heather was recovering on this steep slope overlooking the forestry and was now up to a foot high, but not yet in flower. The bees had to make do with flowers of tormentil and lousewort. Across the lower fringe of the heather slope, there was more outcropping rock, with horizontal strata, where a few layers of rock jutted out to offer a narrow zone of cool shadow. I crawled into one of these lairs. The strata were stacked above me for fifteen feet, like an untidy pile of books. It was a relief to take off boots, socks and shirt and let the cooler air play on my skin; I had a raven's view of the forestry down in the glen.

There was a new noise in the air, not the dishevelled, collapsing and expanding of space as wind rushes around the higher ridges, but a steadier, pervasive streaming noise from the needles and branches of pine trees in the mature stands of plantation. I checked the trees with binoculars but at that distance it was difficult to see movement in the branches; just one or two smaller pines at the edge were swaying slightly.

As the slope bottomed out, in slightly milder conditions,

there was more and more blossom on the bell heather and cross-leaved heath, and black bog rush appeared on the flat ground along with sphagnum mosses, sundew and bog cotton. I found the first stream, a narrow, dark channel swinging through the peat, and here I obeyed Praeger's summons to refresh yourself by total immersion in cold water off the mountain rocks on a hot day. As I undressed, a trout or an eel swirled on the dark surface and red damselflies patrolled the pool margins; nothing in these waters threatened. The footing was firm because of a gritty silt that had washed off the slopes in winter storms and now covered the bed of the stream. When I got out, the disturbed silt, with its grains of gleaming mica, swirled slowly, suspended in the water like a slowly revolving galaxy of stars.

The forestry track was now just a few hundred metres away, and after my bath I tried to follow a path between mature trees and a newly planted area that had earlier been felled; eventually, the going got too soft, so I was forced to follow a line among three-year-old lodgepole pines. If a Zen master were designing a landscape to test my resolve and good cheer late in the day, he could not have done better than this. Every step either bumped against a grassy tussock of purple moor grass or collapsed into a soggy mass of sphagnum. I also had to pick my way around sapling pines and piles of trimmings lying in spiky rows. As there were no sheep here, vegetation luxuriated as deep masses of bell heather in flower, and bright sedges and grasses, with a few spikes of foxglove. I alternated between tussock-floundering and stepping on old ash-grey brash from the felling; it snapped and crackled as I passed. I almost missed the sheep for their efficient stripping back of everything, but there was none within the fenced plantation. It was a relief to reach the forestry track and its guarantee of hard, level ground.

This track ended in a three-kilometre march to meet Fergal at his car. Later that day, I joined Jessica for my first swim in the sea that year and I shouted from a kind of elation of cold.

As spring gave way to summer, bluebells had gone to seed, and the flowers of yellow iris were flying their bright, weak banners in wet places. The wheel of the year was moving towards its zenith at the solstice, and material was being gathered for the bonfires of St John's Eve. Many of the birds had already fledged, and the early impulse of life and fruition was giving way to the high-summer commotion called holidays.

Barr Nead an Iorlaigh
June 20

Jessica and I met my son Seamus with his partner Caoife and son Daniel in Galway on June 19. Seamus gave me a drawing of a sea eagle carrying a fish, based on a photograph of one of the birds at Mountshannon. We set a date early in July for a trip to Mountshannon; the young eagle should be well grown by then and not far from fledging.

Back in Fahy, I spent the next morning putting stuff together for a couple of nights' camping. I was caught between two impulses: the desire to travel light and the need to be comfortably equipped, along with notebooks, maps, binoculars and a telescope. The entire exercise was a micro version of the logistics of big expeditions, which seem to be mainly about shifting astonishing amounts of gear.

When I eventually left at midday, I still had to stop to get food, more camping gas, another map and petrol. Only then could I leave Mulranny and head out across Erris. The arch of the old railway bridge spanning the road near Mulranny has always been for me a ritual passage to something different in terms of space and scale. The novelist Mike McCormack recently described it as a 'subtle shift within me which I always imagined was my soul flinching in the landscape that opened up beyond that bridge, where, within a few miles and with a sudden thinning of the light the mountains withdrew into the clouded distance.'[25] The experience of uncalibrated space is unusual in the west, and it has perplexed many travellers such as Pococke who were accustomed to the romantic sublime of summits, cliffs and waterfalls.

Even Erris, though, has its own stages and markers. There is the road itself, like an installation by Christo, a gesture of pure abstraction that spreads across the unruly surface of the bog from Mulranny to Bangor. Then you pass a tangle of plastic and mesh at the fish farm, rows of turf packed in white fertiliser bags are stacked on the bog; a blue diesel tank survives on an isolated stand from the days when Bord na Móna was harvesting peat on the vast tract west of Bangor. After I left Bangor to go north past Lough Carrowmore, another drama was announced in the makeshift protest signs around the Shell refinery at Bellanaboy: *Shell Hell. Shell Out. Shell's Cops. Shell's Thugs.* An old cottage gable declared, *The Struggle Goes On*, beside the Shell scallop logo. A global struggle was still in evidence: a red minibus parked near the gate was covered in slogans.

A left turn off this road takes you to Rossport, Carrowteige and Portacloy, *An Ghaeltacht Bheo*. This enclave of surviving Irish is one of those cultural reservations that the Irish state has done so much to support over the years. Mine was a typical arrival – a *lá breá* ('fine day'), someone who appears only during fine weather and arrives with a tourist's fantasy of remoteness, cultural purity and authenticity.

The oasis at Portacloy was animated with teenagers from Kildare on an Irish summer camp, their bright kayaks moving across the cove like thin moons of vibrant colours. Their shouts were a happy agitation above the soft noise of lapping water and breaking waves. I thought about moving on somewhere else for more privacy, but I heard a stonechat from a field above the beach, and took that as a sign that I should stay.

On my way I had noticed several eagle pairs on gateposts, near the cemetery outside Bangor, in Bangor itself, and in Portacloy. The eagle pair in Portacloy were cast in concrete, their deep bills and unfeathered tarsi suggesting *Haliaeetus albicilla* (white-tailed sea eagle) rather than *Aquila chrysaetos* (golden eagle). I postulate a subconscious, if not conscious, ancestral memory of eagles in this area as an explanation for these ostentatious figures.

In the evening, after brewing tea, I drove through *Ceathrú Thaidhg* (Carrowteige) with its assertive signs in Irish, to Kilgalligan, which was like an island raised on an altar of light in the evening sun. I heard a commotion of farmyard geese as I parked at the end of a track south of Benwee Head.

I walked to the top of a flat headland, with gulls gliding indifferently on the updraught, and then I heard choughs, six or seven of them in their heraldic pageantry, lifting and tumbling in the air above a cliff face. A few steps more and the brow of a cliff was showing, then an entire bay at my feet 200 metres lower down. There was even a little shingle beach under the highest point. *Barr Nead an Iorlaigh* ('the peak at the eagle's nest') was a site on a map sent to me by Uinsíonn Mac Graith, a local man who had spent years researching and preserving the Irish-language heritage of this area. The traditional eyrie site was unmistakeable: because the strata were twisted and folded here, at one point a curve in the rock layer had created a semi-arch, where lower material had collapsed. This arch was like a hood on the southern side shielding the eyrie from exposure. In the telescope I could see a tiny rock pipit pottering about on the debris of the floor. The ledge was a little more than half way down the cliff, and could hardly have been better designed to prevent access. It looked as though nest material was needed to shore up the outer lip, because the ledge was sloped slightly outwards.

I marvelled at nature's design, which had made an amphitheatre of cliff and a parterre of water for this nest site. Scanning the outer rim of the bay to the south, I saw nothing to rival it.

Rising on the updraught, a sea eagle would have a direct view from here of its neighbours on Achill, at Slievemore and Croaghaun, the top of the Mullet, and eastwards to Benwee Head. From this point, the name of the bay, Broadhaven, came into its own, as a view of dizzying scale and emptiness.

Coming back from Barr Nead an Iorlaigh, I was tempted by a walk towards Kid Island and Benwee Head, but I decided to leave them for the next day and retraced my steps. The open hillside, like the bog below, was a nesting place for all kinds of castoffs, including the bottles from someone's gin habit. Naggin Grave was a name that I added to the area's rich topographical heritage. Bog cotton in the distance resembled newly fallen hail. I was mobbed by a herring gull as I approached the car. In Kilgalligan, New Zealand flax and olearia make impressive defences against the wind.

I stopped in *Ceathrú Thaidhg* to photograph an old stone outhouse, and was jeered by three young lads, who spoke English: 'Hey, mister photograph man, why are you taking pictures?' Then they shouted out in English, 'What's your name?' '*Nach bhfuil aon Gaeilge agaibh*?' I countered. One of them managed the question in Irish. '*Seán is ainm dom*,' I said.

Later that evening, two carloads of youngsters pulled up at the beach while others were hanging about or kicking a ball round the playing field. A couple of the summer-college girls were there in shorts and t-shirts. I thought I was in for a party night and lay in the tent, amused at my own naivety in thinking that I could escape the twenty-first century in the twenty-first century. Music throbbed from a car radio for half an hour, then the girls went back to their *bean a' tí*, and the lads drove off to hunt somewhere else. Three or four others lingered on the beach, in the bright June evening, until midnight. Then I was alone.

Portacloy
June 21

At 8 a.m., the sky was overcast, and there was a chill dampness in the air. Sheep had been around the tent earlier that morning, so close that I could hear a regular ripping sound as they cropped grass. Ravens were calling, and terns were kirricking in the bay.

Shortly after eight, the drizzle increased to rain, and the wind picked up. I read Peter Matthiessen's *The Snow Leopard* for a while until the shower passed and the wind eased. Then a clearance came, and there was even a glimpse of blue.

Stepping out of the tent, I met one of the locals and mentioned my interest in eagles, as well as a place called Spink that I wanted to see. He told me that if I went to the western headland with the old Watch House, I would get a good view of it to the east. Once we had dealt with directions, we switched to Irish; he said that the language was declining in this corner of Erris, as it is in all the Gaeltacht areas in Mayo. There are few houses in Portacloy with children, the old generation are dying off, and the younger set, who have mostly moved away, are not interested in the language anyway. We did not dwell on this topic; I was happy to meet someone who was willing to speak the language and would put up with my hesitations as I searched for a word or a form. Then he quoted the following proverb:

Nuair a thréigfheas an t-iolrach na gleanntaigh,
Nuair a scaipfheas an ceo ar na cnoic,
Ní chaillfidh an sagart a saint
Go dtagann caint ar an bhfiach dubh.

Each line expresses something that will never happen: eagles leaving the glens, clouds dispersing from the hills, priests losing their greed, and ravens acquiring speech. When this quatrain was first coined, it was inconceivable that the glens of north Mayo would ever lose their eagles.

As I followed the newly marked trail out to the old look-out post, *Teach a' Watch*, the cliff face between the bay and the point at Spink gradually revealed itself. Just as interesting was a second headland to my left, running out to sea, parallel to the one I was following. The map marks a promontory fort here at Doonvinalla, known locally as *An Dúna*, and I have read about people going up onto the top of this headland at Lughnasa to pick bilberries and have a party in an ancient ritual that predates the Christianisation of this festival as Reek Sunday in late July. Máire Mac Neill, the great historian of the Lughnasa festival, described the practice as follows:

> It is well remembered that until the beginning of the century a great popular gathering was held there, people coming to it from miles around, not only the boys and girls, but all the active members of the community. The people of the district are accustomed to cliffs and pride themselves on their surefootedness and steady nerves. Many of the visitors from a distance arrived the night before to stay with their relatives in Portacloy. The little village was crowded for the festival. After the midday meal of new potatoes an ascent was made to the Dúna… On the height a fiddler played for the dancers, and the young men competed in jumping and throwing weights. The shebeen-man was there with his jar of poteen from which he sold draughts which added to the general hilarity of the gathering. It was an occasion for romantic meetings.[26]

This practice died out many years ago, and in any case erosion has made the top of the headland virtually inaccessible: the only approach is across a saddle that is crumbling away. An Dúna is on the way to becoming an isolated sea stack without any grazing animals, and in my imagination it will soon qualify as a potential eagle site.

My walk took me out to the 'ÉIRE 63' marker from the Second World War, when they built the Watch House here. The letters 'ÉIRE' are marked here on the ground in quartz, while a border around them has been added recently in the yellowish gneiss of these headlands. The erosion that is making a sea stack of Doonvinalla is also making inroads into this border: one corner was missing on my visit, having fallen into the sea.

I set up the telescope beside *Teach a' Watch* to study the spread of cliffs between Spink and Portacloy. They were over a kilometre wide at this point and fell from a broad plateau at 210 metres. The layers were in three sections: one middle section had even, horizontal layers with a clean, sheer face; to either side there were curves and contortions in the strata. In the area of cliff closest to me, the western section, rock layers curved upwards from the inside to the western extremity, where they ended in loops and convolutions. There was an upper stretch on this face where the drop from the top was not quite sheer and the slope was thick with vegetation; I thought I saw the body of a dead sheep resting where it fell. In my excitement I decided that this broad, grassy patch was the famous site at Spink where breeding sea eagles were recorded by Ussher up to 1909: there was no other feature like it along the cliff, that I could see.

As I examined this area in the telescope, I saw another sheep grazing along this stretch, just a few metres above a hundred-metre drop straight into the sea, and scanning back to the first sheep, I noticed a line of fenceposts in an impossible position above this animal, where farmers had tried to block sheep from going down this terrifying stretch. The thought that men might have gone down this face from the top without harness appalled me; I forgot that cliffwork was an old trade, going back to the days when men collected seabirds from these cliffs for food and feathers, using ropes made from hemp and straw.

Something about that first sheep made me unsure; after a while I saw that it was moving, and that there was a lamb with it, and that the second sheep also had its lamb. What a childhood, to be led by your mother onto the tightest of wind-blown ledges 120 metres above the wrinkling ocean! My admiration for these animals was only exceeded by my awe at the fenceline above them.

A few buzzing finches – twite – flew past me to the tip of the headland and I followed them to the top of the cliff, in my own hesitant and fearful imitation of the fence-makers of the cliff opposite. A fishing launch steamed past with its white statements of foam and seagulls into the bay at Portacloy. This boat had been fishing near the Stags, a few kilometres away.

The Stags of Broadhaven were a cluster of five roughly pyramidal rocks almost one hundred metres high. They had their place for the viewer as a marker, giving scale to sea distance that might otherwise dissolve into a measureless glare. It was impossible to make out their seabird colonies, even with a telescope, from the Watch House where I was standing, but I was impressed at the steep sides of those stacks which Fergal, at my suggestion, had climbed a week earlier to locate breeding Leach's petrel. In the past, ornithologists had camped overnight on the Stags to survey seabirds, and as I trained my telescope on them to figure out where you could possibly pitch a tent on top of those blustery pyramids, I was rueful at the thought that Fergal had run considerable risk to get his evidence of breeding Leach's petrels, the first from the Stags for fourteen years.

At first sight, the sea from such headlands appears as an immense space or emptiness, with little or no boat traffic. It takes binoculars to discover plastic floats marking the position of lobster pots along the coastline or around the stags. Way off in the distance, the only bird I could see with the naked eye was the gannet, but in the telescope I discovered a sea surface busy with cormorants, shags, auks and gulls going about their day's business, moving over the water, or sitting in scattered flocks.

The boat that I had seen approaching Portacloy Bay was dropping off one of the party who had not coped well with the trip. I later found him at the pier, sprawled out on one of the benches, trying to recover from sea sickness. He had no idea where he was, and the directions he had been given back to Belmullet were muddled; I offered to drive him there to meet up with his friends at the end of the day.

After that unscheduled errand I was glad to get back from Belmullet for a few hours' walk in the evening at Benwee Head. The bog road above Kilgalligan brings you almost to the edge of a cliff west of the head with its modern sculpture depicting the legendary children of Lir, who spent part of their time as swans in this area. The tourist sign for the sculpture had three bullet holes from a rifle shattering the perspex cover. One car was parked there, and four walkers were coming back down the slope from the head.

I surveyed the western face of Benwee Head and added two

possible ledges to my survey: in the centre of the face, not far from the top, was a grassy ledge under a ten-metre cliff, with some fresh stone debris because the face above was unstable. There was a second ledge close to the point of the head, an exposed grassy space about ten metres from the clifftop.

Around 1840, Caesar Otway saw young eagles on a number of nests around Benwee Head on ledges such as these, with 'old birds either soaring or perching near at hand.' He declared, 'I never saw so many of these birds at one time, except at Horn Head, Donegal.'[27] One of Otway's companions, a Lieutenant Henri from the coastguard station at Carrowteige, gave details of the eagles' varied diet, of fish taken at sea, grouse, hares and an occasional lamb, making it clear that this coast was once a stronghold of the sea eagle.

Nowadays, there are other predators dominating the vertical faces and the uplifting breezes: I must have walked into the territory of a great black-backed gull, because two of these birds were constantly crossing the space above me; they came so close I could hear the rush of air in their wing feathers and could see their heads swivelling about, as if they were living things separate from the great frames of their wings. They also kept up a constant moaning, like a sound of airy lovemaking. Then the walkers came nearer; their voices carried in the calm evening air, and the noise of gulls was mixed with human voices. I thought someone was calling me, 'Seán', until I realised that it was just the moan of a gull.

Kid Island (*An Mionnán*) is just offshore from here, a little farther west. Its flat top was slightly higher than the headland I was on, and in the evening light a glare of sun flared off the horizon of its pasture. Sheep were grazing on this elevated plateau, and I scanned the steep rocky flanks of An Mionnán to see where a farmer's boat might land; this was puzzling, because the island appeared to be an inaccessible fortress of stone with a slightly curving green roof.

Then I crossed peat workings on the broad headland to get back to the car. The neat, extensive stooks of machine-cut peat, like an art installation, focussed the view in a theatre of water and sky to a dark extract of land. Wheatears were flitting about among them, or were perched on the points, like citizens enjoying an amenity just opened. I was walking there like a visitor to a contemporary art gallery, in silent solitude; somewhere at the edge of my awareness there was another world of insight and memory, stored in a language in decline.

In my modern role as digital cameraman, I stopped in Carrowteige to get a shot of an interesting stone barn, and attempted to open a squeaky gate. The bolt would not slide back, but the squeaking was the signal for a large flock of sheep, bleating frantically, to rush to the gate, thinking they were going to be fed. I thought I had raised the whole village, but no one appeared, and I took my pictures from the roadside.

Sheep were everywhere, especially on the sandy flats and hill at *Corrán Buí* ('yellow crescent'). Their bleating is almost constant in these parts, like an ancestral complaint at the misfortunes of the west, and it does nag at the spirit; but that day I had been in awe of their ability to reach terrifying ledges with barely a tuft of grass between them and the rocks below. Sheep often seem indiscriminate eaters, but a few passed near my tent that morning, eating only the yellow flowers of a hawkweed growing on the dunes. Their grazing motion as they did so was delicate and choosy.

Portacloy
June 22

I slept well, without hearing the rain that fell during the night. After waking at about 7 a.m. I stayed in the tent to write up my journal, to the sounds of choughs and the steady work of waves breaking on the beach. It was as if I had returned to the setting of our holidays as a family in Kerry, on the Dingle Peninsula in the 1970s at an extreme point of land and language. We stayed with an Irish-speaking family near Ballydavid Bay, on the north-western side of the peninsula, where gannets and choughs were living adornments of an essential culture. My mother could speak Irish, and my father knew Irish, but both were held back by a native reticence from making the final, assertive step. We greeted people in Irish, and spoke Irish during short exchanges before returning to English, the language everyone practised with ease. Alongside this tantalising, perplexing Irish vernacular, natural history offered a language that was more gratifying: a series of precise nouns we gathered with our field guides: turnstone, kittiwake, pipewort, tormentil.

I heard an unfamiliar song, and looked out: twites were in the field beside me. These little finches are another precious detail in the vocabulary of Portacloy. The fields in the narrow glen still have a rich meadow flora and are being managed for wildlife by an agri-environmental scheme – the swelling tide of European bureaucracy arrives here just as the Irish language is ebbing. Twites and stonechats, skylarks and meadow pipits, goldfinches and pied wagtails are abundant in the fields along the little stream draining the glen, and they announce a benign new message of biodiversity. The busy twites had broken my spell of concentration so I went for my third swim in as many days, but the water at low tide was icy cold, and I ran back to the rocks after a brief immersion, my flesh tingling.

Then I went to call on the man whose gates were adorned with two concrete sea eagles. He told me that he had seen two eagles high in the air at Spink the previous year in autumn. He was out after sheep and heard an unfamiliar call. When he looked up he saw two eagles turning at height. He knew about the Donegal reintroductions, and he reminded me that you could see Donegal from where we stood. He is another sheep man who seems interested in eagles and is fascinated at the prospect of their return.

After tea and a sandwich, I climbed up the hill to the east of Portacloy, on the Porturlin side. The telescope over my shoulder felt heavy, and somehow symbolic, like a cross, or a grim reaper's scythe. The vegetation was deep and rich: lots of heather and grasses and heath spotted orchids. A small water scheme gathered water from the hill; presumably for this reason sheep had been kept off the hillside and in their absence the vegetation thrived.

This hill is one of two flat tops between Portacloy and Porturlin, with cliffs at their northern side. When I reached the top of the first, I discovered that the ground was quite waterlogged, with black bog rush, which I thought more typical of lowland bog and fen. Here, at this height, and in overcast conditions, the view ahead of me was simplified as open bog and grey sky, with the living sound of skylarks in the air. Only one or two low bluffs punctuate this wonderful altar to the air; I walked round one of them, like a fox, looking for signs of something, and found none.

The map indicated a cluster of small bog locháns, and soon I reached them; they had partly dried out, but there were still some shallow pools, with pond skaters turning on the dark water. An old, rusted sheep fence sagged across the ground, like a careless snare. It was no longer any barrier to the sheep, who ran away, bounding down a scaresome incline, marked by their habitual trails.

I had come past Spink to get a view of the next sweep of this coast, stretching for several kilometres past Pig Island towards the cliffs of Laghtmurragha and the summit of Glinsk. Pig Island appeared as a long, narrow plateau, with steep sides, divided in the middle by a sea arch. Along the top of the outer part, there were some comfortable-looking depressions in the vegetation, partially sheltered by the rocky spine of the island. I made a note of three, and would add one more. Somewhere beyond Pig Island, past the entrance to the port of Porturlin, one more grassy ledge was visible under an escarpment on the shoulder of a sea arch. As I wrote my notes, a tiny trawler, dwarfed by these cliffs and stacks, made its way into the harbour across the glittering water.

Canon Otway, the pioneer of tourism along this coast, gave a memorable account of exploration here in *Sketches in Erris and Tirawley* (1841) and claimed that north Mayo had 'the most magnificent cliff scenery in the British Isles.'[28] He and his local crew passed through the imposing sea arch at Pig Island in a high summer setting of seabird noise:

> What a contrast this gloomy arch presents to all that is bright and sunny in the landlocked bays on either side.

The basalt is black overhead; the sides have no tints save those of sombre ochre; and there is, while your boat is kept stationary, a drop, heavy and fast coming down on either side of you. I am not sure whether the clamour here of the sea birds that were soaring and circling all around… their black, white, blue and grey colours, two or three eagles as it were reposing on their broad wings high overall, and sending out occasionally their lordly voices, which I cannot describe better than likening them to an angry man's laugh, – I say, I am not sure whether all this animal din might not be too much for delicate ears; but in such a place, amidst all the natural grandeur, with every thing in keeping – so savage – it was to me a glorious accompaniment, befitting a scene where man was but a rare intruder on the nesting-place of the oceanic birds, and the home of the eagle.[29]

Like other excursionists, the Canon could articulate his sense of this place with romantic effusion, but on the cliffs east of Portacloy there is an underlying feeling of dispersal, of overwhelming space, which defeats you. I had a glimpse of distance that nothing could domesticate, so I gathered up my stuff and moved back west. Then I came to the edge of the cliff to check the fall and saw that I was close to Spink. At a second approach, I crept forward to the cliff edge where waving bouquets of thrift announced the fall to the sea. Twenty metres under me there was a grassy platform a couple of metres wide under a short, vertical crag. For once, almost uniquely, the grassy slope did not fall away from the cliff face but fell back towards it from a raised lip at the front. From my vantage point I could not see the inside of the platform, but it would clearly have been an ideal nursery for young eagles. They could have pottered about on this platform without falling off, and they had sheltered space here to practise wing flaps before fledging. I was delighted with this extra piece of data and decided to return to base. Then it occurred to me that this had to be the site at Spink that Ussher and Warren documented in 1909 and 1910; the grassy ledge farther west along these cliffs, which was the focus of my searches the day before, might also have served, but it had a more open aspect than this perfect eyrie.

The buzzing of a twite confirmed my feeling that this was the site where native sea eagles last bred in Ireland. I wrote my notes in a small depression in the ground just twenty metres from where the cliff fell away to the sea. The Stags of Broadhaven floated in the distance. A milky haze blurred the horizon, uniting water and sky; the breeze was mild and moderate. The sun was coming through, throwing a shadow from my forefinger onto the page.

In the afternoon, I drove from Portacloy to Porturlin, and was shocked at the untidiness of the fishing port. Old nets and gear were thrown everywhere, in spite of the wealth evident in houses around the narrow bay. Along a farther stretch, from Porturlin back to Belderg, the bog road was cut off from a view of the sea by a series of high headlands, and then by plantations of lodgepole pine. One man was footing turf on a lonely hillside near Srahataggle. At Laghtmurragha, a track into the plantation had a sign saying PRIVATE LAND in large red lettering. Even where space was emptying out with social decline, old boundaries of ownership were still strictly monitored.

After Céide, I stopped at Glenulra ('eagle glen') to take a photograph of Glenulra National School, long since converted into a private house and now for sale.

The Stags of Broadhaven
June 25

The Stags of Broadhaven are the *ultima Thule* of Irish ornithology because they are the only Irish site where the Leach's petrel has been proved to breed. Leach's petrel is a small dark bird that lives on the ocean and comes ashore only to breed on remote islands and rocks at places such as St Kilda and Rona in the Outer Hebrides. They nest in burrows and crevices in these places and are nocturnal at the breeding colonies, so Leach's petrel is probably at the other end of the scale from the user-friendliness of garden birds, which we can watch during the day as we sip coffee at our kitchen table. Birds like petrels and shearwaters are called pelagic species, because of their lives lived on the surface of the ocean outside the breeding season, and for me the word 'pelagic' sums up the strangeness and otherworldliness of nature; during my landlocked life I have only ever visited those grey wildernesses of the northern ocean briefly, and then only with modern gear and provisions to shield me from any real contact with the cold sea. My last swim at Portacloy beach, three days previously, was a brief splash and dash in water I could hardly endure for more than two minutes.

The first time breeding was proved for Leach's petrel on the Stags, a team of scientists managed to land in calm weather and bivvy for a night on one of the rocks, where they located the birds as they returned to the nests to feed their young. During the Seabird 2000 survey, fieldworkers counted 'apparently occupied sites' by playing bird calls and waiting for a response from the burrows. They found a total of 310. Human history has been a slender narrative at the Stags (a lack of fresh water means there is no early Christian settlement here, unlike the Skelligs), but they do crop up in folklore, figure in seabird censuses and are a high-summer destination for angling trips and adventure kayakers. The waters around the Stags are also rich in fish, and attract boats from Ballyglass and Porturlin.

My parents sent me a copy of the first *Atlas of Breeding Birds in Britain and Ireland* when I was living in Geneva in the early eighties. As I check the records for Leach's petrel in the same copy today, there is no full red dot on the map of Ireland to show proved breeding for them, only one tiny dot on the Blasket islands in Kerry where the bird must have been seen or heard, but without proof of breeding. In the species description, several of the locations for Leach's petrel in the Outer Hebrides have Gaelic names: *Eilean Mór* and *Eilean a' Ghobha* on the Flannan islands, while another lonely sea stack off the northern Hebrides, Sula Sgeir, marks the etymology of Old Norse ('gannet skerry'[30]). The Leach's petrel is not just an emblem for the extremity of life in nature, but it also stands for the extremity of human settlement at places such as the Blaskets and St Kilda, and for the poignancy of language at these deserted or uninhabitable rocks way out in the sea.

This visit to the Stags was an instalment of my search of the coast for eagle history, but the boat I hired could take four others, Jessica and three of our friends, so the day became a casual trip around my note-taking and photographing. The RIB had a perspex shield all round, and a large outboard engine as powerful as a car, so our progress on water resembled driving on land. The narrow seats were set forward, and we straddled them like horse riders. Our first run took us from Ballyglass harbour, with its fishing boats and crab boxes, to Benwee Head and An Mionnán, or Kid Island. Well before we got to An Mionnán, the air was teeming with seabirds; I was giving impromptu lessons on the differences between razorbills and guillemots, at the same time puzzling over the appearance of fulmars when seen from below. Then we spotted a pair of great skuas overhead, returning to the green top of An Mionnán; in my old *Atlas* from 1976, great skuas were unknown as breeders in Ireland and since then have become established in a few places. Given that their flight silhouette resembles a buzzard's, my informant at Portacloy may have mistaken these birds for eagles.

When I mentioned my puzzlement at how they got sheep onto An Mionnán, our boatman took us around to the eastern side of the island, where a wedge of rock came down to the water in front of a sheer, banded face of cliff running all the way to the top. This slope of bare rock was the landing place: the sheep could be dropped into the water close to the rock and swim the last few metres on their own. A line of posts ran up the rock from this point, though its purpose was unclear. The pastoral world of grazing sheep was high above us as we moved slowly along, under white-splashed choirs of guillemots and their fulmar angels. The magnificent banding of strata in the rocks, with its twists and buckles, had produced sections in places where only a vault of curved rock remained. On the western side of An Mionnán there were three points where strata had collapsed. One of these was an inverted V rising from the water; another was a dark cave shaped like a lopsided rectangle, also at water level; the third, higher up on that side of the island, was a vault for some sea god, maybe the eponymous Mannanán, to rest in during the worst of the storms. I made note of a niche, in the left corner of this vault, for an eyrie.

Between here and the Stags there were other stacks and rocks that the boatman had to steer carefully around. Each of these had its peculiar geometry, its drapery of weed, and its blush of green and yellow lichen. The Knife. Parson's. Cliara. Other unnamed dark rocks appeared and disappeared under the heaving sea: our boatman pointed these out as places where a boat could be wrecked when the high water covered them and he evoked the vanity of those who went out in new power boats without knowing the coast.

Although they were off my Discovery Series sheet, the Stags were only about two kilometres offshore, and we got to them fairly quickly in the kind conditions. Skeins of puffins rose from the green slopes of the higher, sheltered sections; guillemots scattered from the boat's approach or dived for cover into the grey water. There were four main stacks, formed like pyramids, which time, the sea, bird and plant, had eroded and adorned with life. The lower faces at water level were covered with bladder wrack and limpets; then the grey rock rose to the green life of the top with its plants and bird colonies. We tried to figure out where Fergal had landed from his kayak the previous week, and we pointed and speculated about where you could pick your way up from the water across the knobby sections. Again, it was the layering of rock that gave these stacks their character. Weathering into the layers had produced a mass of protrusions like an egg box, so that, where the slope was not too steep, there were many regular footholds, like a staircase.

Somewhere, on one of these summits, a team of ornithologists camped overnight in 1982 to listen for a Leach's petrel. Before then, I wondered, did a sea eagle ever rear a brood here? I sketched and marked down five possible depressions on the tops, bearing in mind that sea eagles in Norway sometimes nest on the ground on isolated islands if there is no threat of disturbance, but I was haunted by a doubt that all these locations were fearfully exposed. On the other hand, sea eagles had certainly landed there to hunt and get their bearings, like the hooded crow that I saw on the puffin slopes.

Our boat moved slowly among the dark geometry of rock; we passed a young sunbathing seal, well camouflaged on the brown intertidal zone. There were no sirens here to lure us to our death, no Scylla or Charybdis to wreck our boat, so we passed through without incident. The rocks were rich with gull calls, but there were not enough guillemots or razorbills to turn the Stags into an oppressive echo chamber of seabird noise, unlike Downpatrick Head. Puffins were the most numerous auk on the Stags, and they were usually silent; with their comical colours and formal dress they added a reassuring picture-book element to the scene.

As I studied the rocks, smart phones and cameras were busy taking pictures, and I discovered later that we were even being posted on Facebook before we got back ashore. One of these pictures showed me in the bow beside the boatman, looking anxiously around, older than I imagine myself to be. I am now about the same age as my father was when we went to west Kerry on family holidays in the late sixties and early seventies, and watched auks and shags on the busy sea off Slea Head, at the tip of the Dingle Peninsula. There I was in Mayo, over forty years later, caught up with similar wonder, startled by the high-summer commotion of a seabird colony.

The most dramatic theatre of all for the seabird watcher was Skellig Michael, off the Kerry coast; it was too challenging a destination for a young family when I was young, but my father did get there eventually, with a local history society. He was proud of a picture he took, of a tame puffin on the path beside him on the way up to the monastery on Skellig. The picture I have framed in the living room at home is of him at Portacloy a few years before his death, looking at an OS map spread out on the car bonnet. That pose was typical, even in old age he never lost his curiosity about Ireland's wild places, and our move to Mayo in the mid-nineties gave him an entirely new theatre of interest. In many respects, it was another version of that archetype we had known on the Dingle Peninsula in Kerry: a remote place with the Irish language in the daunting setting of the sea.

After the Stags we had a scheduled 'comfort' stop in Portacloy, even though the only facilities were behind the wall of the pier. (On a similar day trip in Italy we were invited to jump into the sea and urinate while treading water.) One of the locals, whom I had met at the weekend, was there at the pier. He offered me another piece of bird lore, about a raven that lifted a cat one day, but the cat bit through his wing and the raven fell back to earth. The concrete pier at Portacloy, he explained, has no proper shelter to deflect the northerly swell, so there is no boat traffic here, unlike at Porturlin nearby. As it now has no practical function, the pier can be admired as a gesture of pure form, an art installation jutting out into the surge of sea waves.

In the afternoon we motored past the cliffs at Spink. This name has taken on mystery and grandeur because of the proximity of eagle ghosts and their followers in the last years prior to extinction in 1909. I pointed out the green tongues of rich growth where the two ewes and their lambs were grazing three days earlier, just above a hundred-metre drop. Our boatman said he gets called out to search this coast for bodies: the cliffs at Céide are sometimes the scene of suicides, and it can take many hours of searching to find the bodies among these crags and reefs. Spink itself rose out of the sea like a Gothic cathedral with several buttresses and extensions. Scanning its nooks and corners for possible eagle homes was made difficult from the sea because of the motion of the swell, and I could not locate the broad, sheltered ledge that I saw on Sunday. Instead, my eye fell on two recesses at the front of Spink like high pulpits in a neo-Gothic church. Nurseries for sea eagles? The exposure here made this idea fanciful. High above us there was an extension from the cliff connecting with part of the stack which had the sheep wire I had looked down on on Sunday. Human intrusion on this feature was precarious and hopeless; much of the wire I saw had been eroded away and lay in pieces on the slope, disintegrating.

East of Spink, another broad curve of coast ran as far as Pig Island. The cliff face here was mostly less precipitous than the first stretch, with a lot of vegetation; in one area, however, the face was perpendicular, with fresh debris from erosion and a small grey beach at its base. The face was scored with long, blackish lines at a forty-five-degree angle in the flesh-coloured rock. There could be no more isolated or inaccessible beach in the country.

One more turn around Pig Island ended our survey from the sea. I added another eagle ledge, on the inner section of Pig Island to the south of the arch that divides it. The marks and sketches in my notebook were overwhelmed by the complexity of this coastline, including the rock cathedral at Spink. I had left my telescope at home because I knew it would be useless in the moving boat, so I was unable to study many ledges, and I thought that there were advantages to peering down and around slopes from the steady footing of headlands.

Pollagh
June 29

The midsummer bonfires of June 23 were cold by now, and two days earlier I saw hazelnuts formed on the trees in the garden. The days were still gloriously bright, but a small instrument had been set in the background to tick away the minutes to the end of summer.

By the time I got to Bangor I could sense the air shifting more rapidly, on the scale of the ocean. The day was clear, the headlands of the north coast rose on the horizon, holding back their cliffs and stacks and surges of foam. I parked just a kilometre before Srahataggle and rested for a while: each time the effort to get away felt greater.

Jessica came with me as far as Mulranny, where she bathed in the sea. She is a confident swimmer and relishes the bite of Atlantic cold. A German tourist thought of emulating her, but he shrieked at the cold as soon as he stepped into the shallows and went no farther.

Pollagh is one of the few approaches to the sea along this sea-eagle coast between Porturlin and Belderg, and appears on the map as the only place where the ten-metre contours are not bunched into a grey shadow to indicate a daunting incline. I had a tent and sleeping bag with me to win some extra time for a look at the cliffs along this stretch. The forecast was for light winds and no rain: good for camping.

After half an hour traipsing across the bog I had a shallow glen on my right, with a few pools fringed with bog cotton. A fox had been stalking birds' nests across the valley floor but left quickly when I appeared; a falcon called from the hillside before flying off towards the cliffs. The sea then appeared for the first time as a gap between two headlands, an inverted triangle of deep gentian blue below the duck-egg blue of sky; the horizon was gin clear; a painter could not have traced a cleaner division between two colours.

I followed the headland west of the little cove, imagining a grassy level around the corner, but the ground got steeper, forcing me up, and when I eventually got a view around the corner, I was hit by depth and emptiness. I crouched down on a precipitous slope, where I might just roll without ending up on the rocks if I slipped, and scanned the cliffs of Laghtmurragha. History helps the mind to focus – sea eagles bred here until about 1900 – but I was still nervous of a void behind me that could creep up and take me down by the shoulders. Laghtmurragha headland has a neat line of fence posts all across the top to within five metres of the edge; the cliff face is not completely vertical, so it has a brown-green covering of vegetation, and from my range I saw seabirds as white specks wheeling across the emptiness. These heights, distances and voids were threatening to defeat me again, as they had near Spink, and I retreated down to the cove to investigate a level area 200 metres away from the sea's edge.

I avoided a soft corner with a carpet of sphagnum and put up the tent in a slightly more exposed, but drier, location, hoping that there would be enough wind to keep down midges. In that narrow pass between headlands there was a wide scree fall on the eastern slope from a few rock escarpments; some rubble dislodged by last winter's storms had tumbled onto the grassy floor of the pass. A few wheatears were stationed on the scree, and I had the usual company of a stonechat.

Sometimes a sheep's bleat in these places can spook me; I was unsettled by the prospect of lying in the tent at night, trying to interpret sounds and shufflings around me. Pollagh was the wildest location I had found so far: just one tiny booley shelter on the way in, an old line of stones at the foot of the scree, and a lobster buoy in the water were the only signs of human presence (plus the contrail of a plane). The forces at work on this coast are awesome: just west of this narrow cove, blocks of stone as big as vans have collapsed from a cliff into a boulder beach at the bottom, and this rock, recently fallen, lies in its raw state on a bed of smoother, sea-worn stones.

One evening, when we were on holiday in Kerry, my father went to Lough Coumasaharn near Glenbeigh in the evening to fish, but he came back early because he had not been able to endure the wild space and solitude of that lonely mountain setting.[31] I thought of him that evening as I tried to settle down for the night and confront that old challenge again.

Calls of birds I knew helped me to find lines of recognition: the screech of an oystercatcher, the yodel of a black-backed gull. Then there was the enticement of strange seabird calls in the darkness to concentrate on, and keep the mind away from other hauntings in the darkness.

I repeated 'the cliffs of Laghtmurragha' to myself as a mantra, as if they were a sacred site of pilgrimage, a place you could look at but not approach close-up. The sign saying PRIVATE LAND was keeping me back; so was a century of eagle extinction, separating me from those cliffs and their eagle lore.

I also thought of Jessica, who would come to Portacloy the next day. I wanted to see an otter for her: otters might come through to bathe in the fresh water of the locháns in the glen, and there were many faint trails in the grass.

Sheep were bleating like disenchanted old men.

Pollagh – Portacloy
June 30

I was woken in the small, almost dark, hours by the growling calls of Manx shearwaters as birds came back to their burrows. The colony at Pollagh is one of the few on the Irish mainland; Manx shearwaters usually prefer rat-free offshore islands as their breeding sites. There were no other sounds, except the tapping of a zip toggle against the fabric of the tent.

In the morning the bay was bright and glistening; two grey

seals with mournful faces watched me as I went to the stream to wash my hands, and twites were buzzing on the headland.

With the morning light in my face, I moved east, climbing above the scree to the more gradual ridges above it. The heather was deep, and the sun hot, making the going arduous. The Stags of Broadhaven began to nudge beyond the cliffs to the west, with the long barge of Pig Island, and, between these two, the cathedral points of Spink.

The ridge gave me a first view into the bay of Skelp. The bay was divided in two by a high, narrow headland. This green arm into Skelp was inaccessible because of a step of cliff several metres high close to the mainland, making for some sheltered hollows on the top of the headland.

As I sat there 150 metres above the sea, with gulls and choughs riding the updraughts, it was difficult to know which way was up or down. Space itself searched for definition in the vast stretch of ocean in front of me: a couple of buoys for a lobster pot, skeins of gannets heading west in search of mackerel, and a single trawler out of Porturlin steaming towards Sligo. This was still all too big; the constant drone of surf on the rocks kept nagging at any definition, it wanted to erode all certainty, even that of geology itself, which was collapsing slowly everywhere. As a reminder of the power of the elements, the previous evening I had found a large plastic fish box over a kilometre from the cove. It had lain there for months, with all the vegetation dead under it, since it had been blown and had tumbled all that way in a winter storm. It was an indication of the loneliness of this place that in all those months no one had come by and retrieved it. The trawler was making good progress towards Sligo – it was time for me, too, to push on.

The inlet at Skelp was similar to Laghtmurragha's, but on a somewhat smaller scale. Much of the cliff was unstable, with slices of yellow gneiss hanging almost vertically and gradually falling into the sea. There were no ledges on these sections of cliff, the faces were sheer, with occasional overhanging extensions. Through the glare, I surveyed the cliffs at Skelp and was at pains to find even one good ledge. The face at Laghtmurragha was similar, but higher, and one corner of it was in a deep recess out of my sight. The west face of Laghtmurragha had cliffs in three ascending sections. Each section leant back from the sea at an angle several degrees off vertical, and the sections increased in size and elevation as you went out. With this face in the morning shade, it was difficult to see any suitable ledges or recesses; it was extremely steep and would not tempt even the foolhardy sheep. On the third, inner section, however, there was a long vertical slit in the face with a loop at the bottom. It looked deep and broad enough to hold a large nest, and it was well clear of the water below. Between this and the second section, a deep notch ran into the headland to a narrow point; in the morning light it had a zone of shadow, like the silhouette of a salmon's tail.

These cliffs have their own story from the time of the Great Famine, of human kleptoparasitism on sea eagles. It concerns a cliffman, who used to take eggs from an eagle's nest at Laghtmurragha and sell them to an egg dealer at Belderg. When food was scarce, he took food from the eyrie and cooked it for his own consumption. He had a further stratagem when the growing eaglet was able to finish the food before he could get to the eyrie. This man stitched up the young eagle's rectum, so that the bird was replete and could not eat the prey brought by the parents. After a time, he unblocked the constriction to allow the bird to recover, and then would repeat the ruse, ensuring a supply of food for himself. The story went that the young eagle eventually fledged, having provided the cliffman with food for some months.[32]

I looked across the bay at those distant cliffs with white seabirds spinning in the air like motes in a snow globe. The bog plants at the clifftop, where I was sitting, were shivering in exposure to the sea, but a few paces back from the edge the bog was like any other, oblivious to gull cries and the deep drop to the sea. I finished my notes and retreated from the sunny oppression of the cliff edge.

As I walked down the slope, the wind jacket tied at my waist fell below my knees. My shadow on the grass was the ghost of a peasant woman moving ahead of me: she had come up to the headland to look out to sea for her fisherman, or had wandered up there in despair at trying to find food since the potato crop had failed. She was a figure full of bewilderment and grief at a destiny that had brought her to such a desperate situation in an unyielding place.

Portacloy

July 1

I came back from Pollagh to meet Jessica at Portacloy, where we camped last night. The wind was brisk from the north, but the pitch on the narrow strip of dunes still served for shelter, and we were even able to cook a meal. Some hot food after a day of anchovy sandwiches was a pleasure.

Jessica swam in the bay, and then we drove around to Benwee Head (*An Bhinn Bhuí*, 'the yellow peak'). I read for a while as she walked up to the top of the headland. It is always surprising how quickly a person covers ground, even at a slow pace: you look away for a few minutes and then you notice the person as a speck moving across the hillside. Jessica stopped to look around her as a kestrel circled overhead. She told me later she had not seen it. Then she was a tiny notch on the headland, giving the place definition, as she did on the beach at Mulranny two days earlier, the first person that morning who had ventured in without a wetsuit. The whole setting of Clew Bay, Croagh Patrick and Clare Island was a context framing her strong figure as she walked out of the waves towards me. 'Matter of fact' this Venus was, like Heaney's bathers in Galway, and just as memorable.

Shortly before dusk that evening, in an agitation of waves and swell, we noticed another agitation: a large pod of dolphins, at least a dozen, in the narrow bay. If they were after mackerel there was more than pure need in their behaviour: we watched them flinging themselves out of the water, performing somersaults over a choppy sea. They appeared to be enlivened by the blustery conditions, just as salmon are spurred into activity when a river rises following heavy rain. They leapt clear of the sea to reclaim the air, which is also the dolphin's element.

After a breezy evening and a calm night, the morning was bright. A sudden burst of sun warmed my face when I emerged from shadow on the way to the pier. Then we went to the Watch House on the headland. The sea was a wall of glitter falling from the sun and we sat to pay homage to this light. The cathedral of Spink was a lofty silhouette within the glitter, and – amazingly – a boat was checking lobster pots under the cliffs. To earn a living in that setting today seemed like a divine calling.

Dolphins were still there, a group of four, plus a couple, arching regularly as they moved towards the headland. Jessica was delighted, as was I. The lobster boat did a turn in Portacloy Bay and intercepted the dolphins close to the headland. A couple of them did a few camera-friendly turns near the boat. Then the boat passed, and the dolphins moved east from where they had come, leaving great, vigorous swirls in the water as they went. All the while, gannets were patrolling the waters in steady, cruising turns, and one long skein of these birds crossed the dark face of the Stags two kilometres away.

The ground we were on, like so much of this coast, is being eroded, and we stared with fascination into the next cove with its active falls of rock and scree faces. At the head of this cove, a boulder beach growled from the breaking motion of surf, and along another section, where the rocks were large and less mobile, the water colour shaded from sandy at the edge to light turquoise a couple of metres away, with waving mops of weed around some boulders.

Later, sitting in the car, we watched one of the farmers leave his house and walk out towards the clifftop, with some fencing material slung over his shoulder, like an archer's quiver; his dog ran across the sloping fields ahead of him, as if he were going to round up the sheep that bunched and scurried about; but that did not appear to be today's task. The farmer walked on, past the dog and his flocks, and did not stop until he reached the edge of the last field at the very clifftop. Here he put down the material he had been carrying and stood on the horizon itself. The gradient was as steep as the side of a pyramid; above the dark ground, the haze of morning was being dissolved by a rising sun. We looked around us for a moment at other things, and when I next looked to the horizon to find him, he had disappeared, gone lower down, I supposed, to follow a line of fencing that needed repair.

For a moment, the man commanded a powerful drama of wild earth, sea, and light, holding his ground at the very extremity of our world; and I saluted him as a bearer of potential and possibility where elements contend.

Burren

July 5

I stood in a grove of spruce trees, well over forty years old, a few of them pushed over by a recent storm. Scolding chaffinches, a family of stonechats. The essence of the place might have been there, in the swaying light and surging rush of wind overhead; I could have sat there for the rest of the evening, without any purpose, and taken my meaning from such a moment, but the huge crag at Burren asked me to continue, despite the risk of being caught by a heavy shower on the open hillside.

Just fifteen minutes from Castlebar, Burren is a sudden piece of raw geology rising out of rolling moorland; this old eagle site is concealed on the farther, northern side of a hill that is rounded and smooth in appearance as you approach from the south. It is only as you pass this modest hill that its drama of scale unfolds.

The highest part of the face is a sheer cliff leaning westwards, with a number of shallow vertical fissures neither deep nor broad enough to hold a nest. To the right, the face has a series of narrow, grassy ledges running diagonally across, and might allow a cliffman to creep in. Among these grassy ledges, to the left of the main face, is a set of rounded points and depressions, with a few suitable recesses, perhaps three in all. The remainder of the face tapers away to the east in a series of outcrops like buttresses below the main ridge. Geology mixes it up with geometry here in a series of overlapping triangles, angles and lines. If Mayo had produced Cézanne, this is the mountain he would have painted obsessively; the forms of these cliffs and outcrops are emerging into the abstract surfaces of Cubism and beyond.

Several years ago, a friend of mine, Michael Kingdon, was collecting folklore relating to the natural world in this area, and he interviewed a local man, Stephen Gillan. When golden eagles were mentioned, the old man told him that his father remembered eagles in the area. The first piece of this informant's eagle lore was taken from literature: 'I read in a book,' he said, 'that when an eagle got old her beak would get so long she wouldn't be able to eat. Then she'd fly off into the setting sun until she was so tired she'd drop into the ocean and drown… Into the setting sun they go, and drown in the ocean.'

The other story has more about it of authentic folklore: 'Down in the village there was a woman had a young child and the eagle came and took the child and took it off to its nest. The very same day Jimmy Mac and some others got an old rope, it was an old rope, all twisted straw, not a nylon rope like you have nowadays. They got this rope and went away to the eagle's nest. Away they went to the top of the cliff and let Jimmy down over the top with the rope around his chest. They let him away down to the nest. The child was alright and he got it, but when they was pulling him back up the rope got jammed, do you see, like it would, and the more it pulled the more it jammed. They pulled and pulled and slowly got them up. When they got them to the top there was just a single strand holding the rope together. Well, Jimmy fell flat on the ground in a fright and his hair went white and he never spoke another word from that day.'

This story, with its motifs of hair turning white through fear and of a rope fraying, is paralleled in an incident highlighted by Maxwell, as he related stories of sea eagles. The anecdote is also the subject of the 1832 frontispiece to *Wild Sports of the West:*

> Two eagles, in the wildest part of a neighbouring county, had for some time depredated on the neighbourhood, and bore away lambs, kids, &c., for the sustenance of their young. Some peasants determined, if possible, to obtain the young birds, and ascended the mountains, but found that the nest was in a part of the perpendicular rock, near one hundred feet below the summit, and about three hundred feet above the sea, which, with terrific appearances, dashed against its base. They had provided themselves with ropes, and a lad, armed with a cimeter, was by this means lowered by the rest. He arrived in safety at the nest, where, as he expected, he was attacked with infinite fury by one of the old eagles, at which he made a stroke with his sword that nearly cut asunder the rope by which he was suspended. Fortunately one strand of it remained… he was cautiously and safely hauled up, when it was found that his hair, which, a quarter of an hour before, had been of a dark auburn, had in that short period become perfectly white.[33]

The phenomenon of hair turning white is meant here as a mark of the extreme fear brought on by such moments, and it also expresses more generally the dangers of *ailleadóireacht*, the trade of the cliffmen who were lowered down these steep cliffs at night in pursuit of seabirds. Maxwell's frontispiece shows a young peasant in a basket mid-air, as heroic as a pikeman of 1798, swinging his curved sword at two attacking eagles, while groups of onlookers in the distance raise their arms in excitement.

Such cliff adventures are unlike the routine dangers of fishing at sea; whereas everyone in these coastal communities shared the hazards of the sea, only exceptional individuals were brave or tough enough to face the cliffs where eagles and seabirds nested. This individual heroism is underlined in the drawing by three distinct groups of onlookers, on a nearby cliff, on a beach at the bottom, and on a large rock, following events near the eyrie. The distribution of people across this vast theatre of excitement makes for an intensely dramatic scene.

The Erris giant Dáithí Bán also gets drawn into these feats of cliff scaling, if we go by a tradition in folklore regarding the site of his fort. It was said that Dáithí Bán, who was famed for his speed, strength and valour, had a fortress on Corslieve at Coire na nGarú. This tradition locates Dáithí's fort, not at the cairn on top of the mountain, but on the side of a cliff in the most dramatic corrie of all, Coire na nGarú. It was said that the door of this fort was on the cliff face, and people went down there on ropes, having fixed them with iron stakes at the top, but they failed to force the doors open. In this account, there is some confusion or crossover between this fortress in the cliff at Coire na nGarú, and the customary site on the summit of Corslieve, the great cairn, Leachta Dháithí Bhán.[34]

Dáithí's whiteness is intriguing, in view of both the whiteness effected on the hair of the cliff climber by fear, and, I believe, the white tail feathers of sea eagles. (Mature sea eagles can also be conspicuously pale about the head and shoulders.) In this tentative reading of a tradition of hair being whitened by the terror of eagle cliffs, I sense the pale colours of sea eagles playing their part, infusing the hair of eagle hunters, and giving a legendary pallor – and even a dwelling on the cliff face – to the greatest of Erris giants.

As these stories pass out of hearing, along with storytelling itself, we have to look elsewhere for ancestral memories of eagles; on my way back to Castlebar I find some, just a few kilometres from Burren: two large, white plaster eagles on gateposts at the entrance to a house.

Eagle Bay, Mountshannon
July 7–8

The news from Mountshannon, on Lough Derg in County Clare, was very encouraging. The first successful sea eagle pair from 2013, which had fledged two young, now had a new nest with a single chick on a different island. The waters of Lough Derg were rich in fish, the densely wooded islands in the bay were secure, and the birds seemed to tolerate a certain amount of boating traffic. This was reason enough for us to justify a trip, but I also had a literary engagement in Cork, and an old obligation to revisit Kerry with Jessica, so we set out for an extended July break in the south-west.

Our campsite at Mountshannon was on the lakeshore, with a view across the water to Inis Cealtra and the north Tipperary hills on the opposite shore. This was memory territory for me: occasionally, our family would come up to Lough Derg for a boat trip to go fishing or sightseeing; when I was a student I came here to visit a girlfriend who was working on a dig with Liam de Paor at Inis Cealtra – and I almost drowned on a foolish attempt to swim to an island. On another occasion at Mountshannon during the mayfly season the lake and lakeshore were thick with the famous insects. As I scanned the lake for sea eagles, it occurred to me that natural history or science – even my amateur approximation to science – is the negation of memory. Grebe, tern and swan are distractions from the past and its sadness, loss and memories of wonder.

When I looked up from writing the last sentence, a swan came paddling strongly towards me and looked for an offering, which I did not give. The great white bird contradicted what I had just written by its sheer presence. It could be saying, 'You are wrong to treat me as a piece of mere data. I also come from the visionary world.'

I woke at 7 a.m. There had been heavy rain in the night, which woke us. After it stopped, I could hear the peck and patter of drops on leaves, and, once, a ghostly sound as a nocturnal walker passed close to the tent. When the drops of rain had drained away, there were just sounds of lakewater lapping against stones, and then, soon after 3 a.m., swallow calls over the water as a few birds ventured out in the darkness.

Our campsite turned out to be very close to the nest on Cribby Island. We called in at the viewing hut that they had just opened at the harbour and realised that their telescope was trained on an island 200 metres past the point where our tent was pitched, so that evening we walked through the campsite, along the shore, past one chalet playing mellow music, and set up the telescope.

I quickly had a fix on the nest, in a large Scots pine at the edge of a thickly wooded island with a fringe of reeds all round. I could see the eaglet's pale head move briefly, a tiny pale speck among the pine needles; the nest itself was scarcely visible because of growth. We watched that point for a while but did not notice any more movement. Around dusk, the wind fell, and all light seemed to have gathered on the surface of the water's mercury glow. We decided that there would be no more eagle movement for the day and walked back along the shore to the tent. Sedges were skating across the water, bringing a few trout into the shallows to feed.

The next morning, overnight rain had passed, and there was a rough jabble on the surface of the lake. I went along the shore with the scope and set it up to view the nest. At about 8 a.m. one of the adults flew away to the left, across the treetops. The chick was preening in the bright morning sun. The head feathers were well formed, giving a rich, dark-brown crown. The chick looked alert and inquisitive, reacting to movements of smaller birds in the tree canopy.

Later that morning, after a run to Limerick to pick up our grandson Daniel, we were back at the lake with the telescope on the nest. One of the adults was perched to the left of the nest, the chick presumably supine (I later discovered that he had been tagged that morning); then the adult took off, and a second adult appeared. This bird landed on a branch with a prey item – which looked to me like a barn owl. It dumped this on the nest, and the chick proceeded to strip it and eat. The first adult flew to another tall pine farther to the right, where it was mobbed by a herring gull.

The sight of two adult sea eagles in flight, with the white wedge-shaped tail of mature birds, was inspiring. The eagles in flight were set against a backdrop of sky and upland on the

Tipperary side of the lake. In their wild, yet precarious state, they are a glorious presence in the area, and their existence gave me new ideas that took getting used to: 'sea eagles are now breeding in County Clare'; 'sea eagles are seen regularly on Lough Derg'.

Caught up in these long-sighted thoughts, I had forgotten my grandson: he was standing at the other end of the telescope, looking at me. When I dropped him back to Limerick in the afternoon, I discovered two eagle images in stained glass on either side of the front door of his house. Seamus had been too busy with his own life to notice these motifs. The deep yellow bills of these eagles said sea eagles to me.

When I went back to the viewing point that evening I met Nigel Beers Smith, who had been watching the Mountshannon sea eagles for a few years. Nigel had an elaborate array of high-end equipment in place to observe and photograph the birds. We chatted for a while about sea eagles. A second pair was holding territory near Portumna, at the northern end of the lake; and he shared with me a rumour of another pair on Achill island.

Eagle Point, Bantry
July 9

The visit to Mountshannon and Limerick had me thinking about the passage of time: the trip onwards to Kerry and west Cork would mean for me a return to some places after a gap of nearly forty years. Wordsworth dramatised an interval of five years in 'Tintern Abbey' – I wondered how he might have dealt with forty.

I lay awake beside the lake at 5 a.m. listening to rooks, pigeons, swans and a blackcap: these sounds were the same before me, and would be the same after me. I felt a detachment from this world because of the passage of time; even Wordsworth's link with the past faded as he got older and was drawn to the consolations of the spirit. The objects of memory themselves become ghostly, and drift away from the places that held them. Limerick is not a theatre of the past for me any more. My visits are short. Sometimes I drive past.

It was frustrating to spend a whole day at the wheel with so much wild country flashing past as *scenery*, and no time even to look at it because of the need to watch the road. We stopped only at Ladies' View above Killarney to enjoy the view back over the lakes. The mountains here are rocky, with woodland and grass cover, and are not clothed in blanket bog; the oak woodland gives an eighteenth-century picturesque feel of antiquity, as if the landscape itself conformed to painterly Romantic history. As we drove on to the pass, a deer at the roadside seemed to be part of the same ornate pattern.

That evening at the campsite, we were told about a failed breeding attempt at Garinish Island near Glengarriff that year. As we were pitching the tent, a family group walked past. A little girl pointed to a large gull, 'Mammy, is that an eagle?' And indeed, large gulls in the distance made you look twice.

Eagle Point
July 10

The campsite at Eagle Point looks out on a mussel farm, where a boat was working among the rafts. A dull, repeated thump of working machinery came across the water to fill the morning as people stirred from their tents and mobile homes. It was as if I had fallen asleep on a childhood holiday in the seventies and woken up to a new country, with an affluent new generation. Part of the novelty of that feeling was our anonymity: as a child you are met in the company of your parents, who have announced you beforehand as Paud and Noreen's son, Mattie's nephew, Liam's brother; at the age of fifty-six I was in a campsite, unknown among strangers.

Last night I texted a friend about childhood associations and the places in west Cork we were planning to visit after the poetry reading. I thought that revisiting those places might allow me to get beyond a kind of nagging sadness at the passage of time and replace it with new feelings. I was perplexed by the notion in Wordsworth that memory is an ineluctable truth, a powerful restorative. This idea has a long history in literature, culminating in Proust's *A la Recherche*, not to speak of its role in psychoanalysis. But it cannot, I imagine, be the only truth. Some writers and thinkers operate with ideas and forms that have no ostensible reference to memory; this is obvious in the case of scientific work, but it also occurs as a guiding influence in art and philosophy: the principle of free thought in Socrates, Warhol's empty spaces, Naumann's zip paintings. It can be harder to locate in literature, but John Banville is one instance of a writer who until recently resisted personal reminiscence, withdrawing from his work as much as possible.

One thing that the focus on memory tends to contradict is the reality of change. If we were only the sum of our recollections, then nothing would ever change in us, just the process of revelation as we came to recognise earlier layers of association and their truths. At other moments, we are conscious of difference, the remoteness of the past, our distance from it, and that a new awareness is delivered by the present. Such occasions are an opportunity for liberation, even into a space that is empty or abstract, with all of the possibilities that that implies.

When I was on Garinish Island as a kid, as we got on the boat for the return trip, I saw a foreign couple sitting in the sun, openly cuddling and petting each other, and thought this was an extraordinary, transgressive luxury. Their foreignness was clear from their open behaviour, their self-confidence, and their unquestioning joy in each other. They were unclouded by the shadow of hesitation and guilt that stalked my experience growing up. Now I categorise that moment of my own coming of age as a taxonomist does, and put it away in an archive, without feeling any connection.

I read that afternoon at the West Cork Literary Festival with Vona Groarke and David Wheatley. About sixty people were there, a good turnout for a poetry reading. In the evening we attended a session on literary memoir with Blake Morrison and Hugo Hamilton. The event was in the same room, but they had opened a screen at the back to make a much bigger venue and accommodate about 200 people. It was a perfect demonstration of how the readership for poetry stands in comparison with the readership for prose memoir.

Bantry
July 11

A comfortable bed and a hot shower were great pleasures after three nights under canvas. The hotel was thronged with up-and-coming writers discussing manuscripts and projects. One London literary editor was holding a consultation clinic; each person on her list got a forty-five-minute appointment. A portion of the literary metropolis had decamped to Bantry for a week. The atmosphere was busy, competitive, professional.

The main square in Bantry was crowded with a Friday market. A large number of traders were there, many alternative types from the area selling locally grown, locally made, the people Derek Mahon refers to as 'yoghurt weavers'. There were also Asian traders selling clothes, and a few travellers selling hardware. Westport has tried this, but Mayo lacks a critical mass of alternative producers and craftspeople, and the blustery weather conspires to frustrate trading in the open air.

We drove out along the Beara Peninsula towards a Buddhist centre, following the campsite manager's recommendation to Jessica. When we got there, after an hour of driving, the centre was closed for a retreat; we shrugged and smiled at this test of our spiritual resolve.

The geology of the peninsula is very harsh: great, thick layers of rock lying at upright angles; only around Allihies does the rock change into a narrow-banded formation, and this translates as a pleasing design in old walls and outhouses. Many of these are restored, as people come to appreciate older ways of building and wish to honour the anonymous craftsmen who made these fine structures.

We camped that evening between Castletownbere and Glengarriff, close to the sea. After a noisy family from Cork had finally gone to bed, we could hear calls of curlews from the shore.

Glengarriff
July 12

The tent and grass were drenched with overnight rain. Curlews were still calling. I roused myself to get a few things ready for breakfast and the trip to Garinish Island, which I visited over forty years ago with my family.

The Blue Pool ferry leaves from Glengarriff, at a narrow inlet formed by the mouth of a river running into the sea among large, bus-sized outcrops of rock. At low tide, these rocks surrounding us were heavily bearded with flowing bunches of yellow bladder wrack. The ferry nowadays has an elaborate wharf with a steel and concrete landing stage designed for wheelchair access; the boat is covered and the helmsman's steering wheel is housed under a canopy in the bow. One of the boatmen stood on the wharf with a mobile phone and checked the arrival of more customers.

We left the inlet of the Blue Pool and motored slowly through the heavy inertia of the bay, where seals and their pups were hauled out on rocks. The day was overcast and damp, the islands heavily wooded and thick with rhododendron. As we approached Garinish Island along its eastern arm, our boatman slowed down: right there above us was this year's eagle nest in the fork of a pine and there were the eagle pair with their tags, sitting on branches a few metres away. Their heads and upperparts were not as pale as the Mountshannon birds, as they were younger. We were told that they had not been seen for three and a half weeks. There was much interest in these birds among the people on the boat. The eagles did not fly, although we were only a short distance away. Another man on the boat had seen the birds at Mountshannon and related the story of a clumsy attempt to cut branches and mount a camera near the nest on Bushy Island the previous year. I had read about this and the 'negative' reaction it provoked in the birds. Our newly arrived eagles were suffering from popularity and I hoped that people would learn to manage this without intruding on the nesting pairs.

Fortunately for the eagles, the Garinish Island gardens are now in the care of the state's Office of Public Works and the site is well protected. The gardens are like a piece of Italy, with oriental and Greek influences, established in West Cork. The original owners, Annan and Violet Bryce, were drawn to Garinish as gardeners by the mild, moist, almost sub-tropical climate in this sheltered corner of Bantry Bay. They then hired a gifted architect, Harold Ainsworth Peto, who brought his own neoclassical taste to the island; Jessica and I wandered around the blue-tiled pool in front of the 'Casita', a pavilion that could have been designed for the de Medicis, with additional suggestions of a Japanese tea house. We marvelled at the detail of the capitals in the colonnade, an Arts and Crafts take on the Ionic order, in bright cream Carrara marble. Then I chatted to one of the gardeners about damage to the gardens from the winter's famous storms; he told me that they were relatively unaffected by the great cold a few years earlier.

As we walked further into the island, we came to a grassy avenue among the trees, which is the image of the gardens I remember from childhood. The avenue led us to a flight of steps to an open, Greek-style temple, with a view through trees onto the bay, and then, returning down the same steps, a sign directed us to 'Happy Valley'. As we walked among the pines, cedars and eucalyptus, I caught a heavy tropical humus smell, which I first experienced in the large, central section of the glasshouse at the National Botanic Gardens in Glasnevin. These, along with the Zoo and the Natural History Museum, were places of wonder for our family on visits to Dublin. My father brought us to those institutions to make us understand that Ireland's identity was as much about the country's flora and fauna as it had to do with symbols of the armed revolution such as you get at the Garden of Remembrance in Parnell Square, and the Cuchulain statue in the General Post Office.

Later, as we sat in the Italian tea house, I was looking directly at the spot where that couple were fondling each other all those years ago. At that moment, I had glimpsed a place of joy and affection that I had never witnessed among my own people, and that I did not think would ever be offered to me.

On another stroll through a walled section of the gardens we chatted about the sea eagles we had seen in Norway. Then we heard a sound, which Jessica likened to a sheet being shaken out, and we saw one of the eagles flying low overhead; in a few moments the bird was circling much higher up, like a vulture. It continued to gain height and then vanished. I said, with a flourish of patriotic pride, 'Great to see this in an Irish sky.'

Glengarriff – Lauragh
July 13

Sun warmed the tent in the morning; its appearance after a few grey days felt like a special gift and the walls of the tent were glowing. I lay in my sleeping bag listening to a little stream running past our pitch and a blackcap singing in the wood. There were other calls and songs: robin, wren, a raven overhead, and juveniles of species that I did not recognise.

This was the best pitch we had had that week, on a narrow terrace of green between a long ridge of rock and a stream running off the rocky hill, hurrying through mixed woodland of willow, birch, oak and pine. The site was sheltered and quiet; the elements and weather agreed. I opened the tent flap to watch blue sky framed by pine and birch branches, and closed it again after a while to keep out midges.

We ate breakfast beside a large rock at the edge of another terrace next to our own. Bees were buzzing in the brambles, and I noticed large, fully-formed hazel nuts in the growth overhead needing only time to mature them into Keats's plenty. We were over 300 kilometres south of Westport, enough to add an extra pulse of warmth and fruition to the earth. The previous day on Garinish felt like being in Italy. The site was so pleasing that we decided to stay another night.

The geology and terrain opened up further as we explored the peninsula later that day; the weather had largely cleared to reveal Hungry Hill and other stony peaks. The geology was starker than anything I had seen before, with the exception of the Burren in Clare. As on the north Mayo coast, the strata have been pushed by pressure in different directions:

sometimes they lie horizontally, sometimes vertically, but more typically they lie at an angle between these extremes. The ridges often resemble a sliced loaf of bread that has slumped to one side. The strata are thick, several feet thick in many instances, and the underlying rock emerges everywhere as ridges like whalebacks, pyramids and odd trapezoidal forms.

On the Beara Peninsula, the entire landscape is outcropping rock rising to the surface. Farming has won back a cluster of fields and meadows here and there, but the farmer's tractor often moves among iceberg shapes and pyramids of rock as he cuts silage, and sheep browse the grassy lines among cracks in the rock strata.

The most spectacular valley of all is on the northern side of the Healy Pass running down to a sea inlet at Lauragh. Glanmore Lake shimmered under us as we pulled in to relish the view. The floor of the glen is made up of stands of conifer and broadleaf woodland, with several clusters of green fields where a few farmers have gone against the rocky grain and created some grazing. Many of these fields are invaded by rock forms, and the slopes above are littered with blocks of stone from higher escarpments still breaking up at their own pace of centuries. Incredibly, three rectangular fields the size of football pitches stretch up the mountain where, some time in the nineteenth century, people were given a pittance to gather loose stones from the slope to make walls. As we looked down on this scene, a local man greeted us, and within a few questions he knew how long we had been married, how old Seamus and Daniel were, and what we held to be most important in life. Health, we said, and that reassured him.

As we were parking at a coffee shop in Lauragh I saw a large raptor above a group of pines near the shore. Buzzard was my first, cautious thought, but then the bird lowered its feet as it descended, and I could see two huge talons forming its landing gear: we were sure that this was another sea eagle from the Kerry programme. It landed in the pines and straight away sent up a large gull, which started to complain in a shrill clamour.

The pines at Lauragh are crowded along a rocky ridge across a narrow, wooded inlet. Two herons and a little egret were prospecting for food by the water's edge. On another day, these three birds would have been wonderful in themselves, but their wildness was crowned by the bird we had just seen, now sitting in one of the tall pines, taking the sun on its feathers, waiting for mullet to enter the shallows on the rising tide, where they would be easy, conspicuous prey.

Our eagle tally so far that week: two adults and an eaglet at Mountshannon; two adults on Garinish; one bird at Lauragh, in Kerry.

Killarney
July 14

Next morning, rain came in pulses of heavy drizzle interspersed with periods of steadier rain. The night had been very mild, and then the whole world surrendered to the fact of Atlantic rain. The mobile homes and tents were quiet; just a few people carried on the rituals of civilised life, scuttling to the shower rooms.

I imagine that this rain is different from rain in the north-west. Among the mountains of the south-west, combined with the mildness of the coast, rain seems finer, closer to drizzle. During our holidays on the Dingle Peninsula, this drizzle would set in for days at a time and all normal holiday activities would be suspended.

Now that I have been watching rain for several years in Mayo, as sea trout angler and as a gardener, I do not recall this mist very often. Although we are not far from the coast, the winds are stronger in Mayo, and the aspect more open, so that rain blows through more quickly. Added to that is the fact that, with far fewer trees, damp air is less likely to linger. My own oak plantings at home have to cope with the aggression of winds, but they are making progress; as they mature and create more shelter, I imagine less agitation of air around them, with dampness lingering in the branches and the oak's great associated flora of lichens and mosses beginning to emerge.

As we left Glengarriff, we got a view of its lovely oak woods. Jessica had to brake sharply when a pine marten made a dash for it across the road just a few metres in front of the car. The animal's appearance confirmed the richness of these woodlands and we greeted it as an auspicious sign for the day. On this occasion, we did not visit the woodland reserve at Glengarriff; my brother and I did camp there once in the eighties, and we watched woodcock roding over the canopy at dusk.

We followed the road to Kenmare over the Caha mountains and stopped at Tulloha National School to photograph a large painting of a sea eagle on the front of the building. The principal here must have had a great connection with wildlife, because the entire façade of the school was covered with depictions of deer, otters, seals and birds in landscape scenes. And in Kenmare, we saw an advert for wildlife cruises in Kenmare Bay that highlighted seals, dolphins and eagles.

We reached Muckross House in the afternoon and had a picnic in the park, among the trees. Rooks approached very close and we rewarded them with cheese scraps. One rook couple were particularly caring, searching the feathers on each other's heads for mites and ticks.

Jessica felt emotional again, thinking of her father, who had been in Killarney on holiday twenty years earlier and gave Jessica her love of camping.

'Why have you never brought me here?' asked Jessica, and I replied, saying something about how Killarney was my parents' haunt, and when I was younger I needed to find a different place, a territory of my own. She was stunned by the beauty of Muckross House and its location.

Once we had crossed the lawn between the house and the lake, we left most of the visitors behind. It was as if we were walking into an eighteenth-century painting or engraving. The lakeshore had steep rocks rising from the water for a couple of metres, with a dense covering of trees and shrubs. Beyond these rocky margins, the slopes and spurs higher up were densely wooded, and the entire scene was dominated by high mountains. I was in awe of the situation, and of the fact that someone once *owned* this setting, with its mock Tudor mansion, and that the entire estate was eventually gifted to the Irish nation.

We emerged from the canopy of trees onto the lakeshore, scanning the sky for eagles. I watched a large bird circling far up, but without binoculars I was not sure and concluded that it was a gull. The setting appeared superb for eagles, but eagles cannot feed on scenery, and many of the released birds had dispersed from here. They were now roaming over open countryside and coast – and their fortunes would be shaped by the whole gamut of indifference, wonder and suspicion that their appearance in a landscape elicits. The magnificence of the Killarney setting belies the destructive attitudes that still obtain in some places.

The trees on the peninsula below the house were a wonder: great oaks, yew trees, arbutus, beech and pine. Many huge limbs had come down onto the path following the mighty storms of the previous winter – great crack, we joked – and in one place the path was still blocked by fallen tree trunks. These big oaks were a picture of antiquity, monarchs of woodland, emblems of statehood and secure constitutions. The legacies of painters like Caspar David Friedrich and thinkers such as Edmund Burke were still alive in the area. But on that occasion we could see a new phase of oak history: many of them had fallen in the winter storms, and on that peninsula it was clear that the oaks were declining. The National Parks and Wildlife Service, in their wisdom, had planted Scots pine in the clearings, but there were no signs of oak regeneration. The old trees, including yew and arbutus, were no longer thriving: the exposure here was presumably too severe, and oak was being superseded by Scots pine.

Killarney
July 15

The campsite came to life gradually in the morning, in its own slow holiday time, despite the fact that we were close to a busy main road. There had been traffic noise since 6 a.m., a sign that we were squatting at the boundary of other people's lives. Most of the campers and caravaners did not engage beyond the merest greeting. I passed them on the way to the kitchen and the toilets and it was clear that they had no desire to be disturbed from their personal space. We were all outside the narrative of lives and nations. I had scarcely seen a newspaper all week. Germany had just won the World Cup, but none of the Germans I saw seemed excited by it; just one German flag was flying at the campsite in Glengarriff.

Later that morning, I discovered that Killarney was bigger than I remembered, and that the kitsch tourist version of Ireland was still thriving. It took me a lot of walking through busy streets to find the tourist information office, buy an OS map, and book a boat trip for the next day. By the time we parked at Torc waterfall, outside the town, I was impatient to get away from the crowds. We marched smartly up the slope to the waterfall, which was only a shadow of its winter self. The storms had brought down tall Scots pines, and their upended roots had torn up rocks and soil; some of this debris was lying in the gorge of the stream, while in other places large boles, which were straddling the path, had been cut through, to allow walkers to pass. Storms and climate change deliver a new version of the Romantic sublime, overwhelming our certainties.

We stopped by Muckross Lake to picnic as the wind picked up and drove waves ashore in our direction. I said to Jess that we could have had eagles overhead all morning, without seeing them. I think that the waters of the Killarney lakes are less prolific than the sea inlets near Glengarriff and Kenmare.

At Dinis Cottage, the oaks along the lake were also in decline: birch, holly and rhododendron were coming through, but no young oaks. I finally had a decent map and noticed eagle place names all over the region. While this is a magnificent area of mountain and woodland, there was a doubt in my mind that the Reeks were not typical sea eagle country. The release site in Killarney National Park has visible grandeur, and sea eagles would be a great adornment over the lakes and mountains, but they have probably dispersed from here to richer habitats along the coast. Something similar happened in Scotland, where sea eagles left the release site on the island of Rhum and moved to better habitats on nearby Mull.

We left Dinis Cottage by boat and motored back to Muckross. The wind set up a strong jabble on the water and we scanned the skies, in vain. The boatman told me that they did not see eagles as often as before, and that the food dumps had been discontinued. He said that two pairs were established in Killarney National Park, and he also knew about the Glengarriff pair.

Killarney – Caherciveen
July 16

The boat trip we had signed up for was one of the classic Killarney journeys, from Ross Castle on Lough Leane, to the Upper Lake, via Eagle's Nest and the Long Range. The open lake boat held twelve of us in bright life jackets, plus our talkative boatman with his rapid-fire stock-in-trade of lake district yarns and tall tales. The first stage of the trip took us past Innisfallen, onto the great stretch of open water under Tomies and Shehy mountains. The slopes under Tomies and Shehy were magnificently wooded, but rhododendron had made huge inroads, and the darker oaks looked as if they were sinking into a yellow-green mire.

Our boat scraped the bottom of the stream under Brickeen bridge at the entrance to the middle lake, and we were asked to move forward to aid its passage. After Dinis Cottage, everyone was asked to leave the boat and walk beyond Old Weir bridge, except for myself. I was enlisted to help the boatman haul the boat against the river current along a shallow stretch where the Long Range runs into the middle lake. And I was even jumping about with ropes at his command. This exercise is unchanged since it was first described by John Bush, one of Killarney's first travel writers, in the 1760s.[35]

When we had helped the others back onboard, we continued through a long channel towards the Upper Lake. This took us close to Eagle's Nest, a high outcrop of rock very similar in outline to Spink. The eagles that lived and bred at this site were being noticed by poets and excursionists from the mid-eighteenth century. In his picturesque poem

Killarney (1769), Joseph Atkinson celebrated the beauty and sporting pleasures of the area, but called for the destruction of the eagle:

> Behold, yon awful precipice arise,
> From thence the Eagle gives his race supplies!
> From thence stupendous, wings his soaring way,
> Or furious darts upon his helpless prey:
> Should he come near – ah, fire thy vengence fierce!
> Blest, if thou canst the greedy tyrant pierce:
> Then from his bosom all his vitals draw!
> No more to keep the feather'd World in awe.[36]

This poem also described the echoes produced in these mountains by French horns that were sounded during the stag hunt; even more impressive, according to Charles Smith in his 1756 account of *The Antient and Present State of the County of Kerry*, 'are those made by the discharge of cannon placed in a proper situation, upon the points of some particular islands, which may best answer to the concave sides of the mountains.'[37] Nearly seventy years later, G. N. Wright's *Guide to the Lakes of Killarney* (1822) makes it clear that cannon were still being fired to entertain tourists at Eagle's Nest, and that birds were still in situ:

> It is from this sublime and stupendous rock the sound is
> returned in so miraculous a manner, that it is considered
> one of the most singular phenomena in existence. A small
> hillock on the opposite side of the river, usually called
> the "Station for Audience," is used as the resting place of
> a paterara, which is carried in the boat from Killarney:
> the gunner is placed on one side of the hillock, and the
> auditor on the other, and upon the discharge of the piece,

a roaring is heard in the bosom of the opposite mountain, like a peal of thunder, or the discharge of a train of artillery, and this echo is multiplied a number of times, after which it gradually fades away, like the rolling of a distant thunder. The exact residence of the eagle may be distinguished by a black mark near the vertex of the rock, and the noble inhabitant is frequently seen soaring above the heads of the passengers on the river, and directing their admirable gaze towards his inaccessible retreat.[38]

I noticed that rhododendron had encroached onto the sheer slopes even here. We were all eyes as we moved through the Long Range. A salmon splashed on the surface ahead of the boat and a young hind appeared, browsing on the shore. Jessica poked me gently to tell me how much she was impressed by the scenery. As we left the narrow channel to enter the Upper Lake, I checked my map: all the islands on the upper lake have picturesque English names: Stag Island, Arbutus Island, Juniper Island, Eagle Island. Killarney's landscape has been fully domesticated by tourist associations, and by the legacy of Queen Victoria's visit in 1861: Queen's Cottage, Prince of Wales Rock.

Our boatman pointed to the treetops on Eagle Island and said that the eagles regularly perched there. This behaviour again confirms the place name: old, decayed branches protruded from the canopy, ideal perching posts. 'Once an eagle island, always an eagle island.' This, together with the sight of salmon in these waters, and deer along the lakeshore, confirmed Killarney in my mind as one of the finest places in the country, along with the Burren and the Aran Islands.

On our return leg, another salmon jumped in the Long Range and a fisherman passed in an open lake boat, trolling for salmon with four lines. The setting was spectacular: tremendous combinations of crag, escarpment and woodland. We again had to leave the boat at the narrow stream, but I had no job hauling this time as the boat was going down with the current, not upstream against it. We all walked through woodland and deep Calluna heather, still wearing our bright-orange flotation aids, like a group exploring a strange new planet. Some of the older Americans were very frail and had difficulty on the rocky stretches of the path: I brought up the rear, to ensure that none of our elderly companions got left behind.

As we approached Ross Castle at the end of the trip, there was a sight to complement the old, romantic engravings: a group of bright-red and -yellow kayaks, like a flock of birds, sitting in the lee of a large rocky islet.

We left Killarney for Caherciveen later that afternoon, shaking off the crowds. The mountains west of Killarney with their covering of blanket bog began to resemble Mayo's smooth, rounded mountains. Then I noticed sheep on the slopes, the first of those destructive animals I had seen for a few days. I was scanning the sky again, thinking of GPS records of eagles from the Glenbeigh and Lough Caragh areas. The dark recess of Lough Coumasaharn was a few kilometres away to our left; I remembered its awesome, forbidding cliff falls from my childhood. Other early memories were stirred on that evening drive: fishing for little black trout in streams and in remote mountain lakes such as Coumasaharn and Acoose, swimming at Kells Bay and Rossbeigh, and seeing ravens for the first time in the mountains above the large, disused railway bridge near Caherciveen.

Mannix Point, Caherciveen
July 17

People began to say, 'The summer is flying by,' there being a wish in us to see it pass, but we were able to walk along the shore at 10 p.m. before dark the previous evening, and we did not need lamps or torches at all. The evening was calm and fine; then the wind picked up overnight and rattled our tent early in the morning.

The campsite was quiet, people were still cocooned in their shells of privacy. Grey cloud was down on the hilltops and the wind created a noise about the place to drive you indoors. The panoramas of the previous day were shut down and weather set us into a different mode: to hear stories, see fine craftwork, drink tea or coffee, prepare gear for the next stage.

We were breakfasted and ready to go by nine, as the younger people around us were still emerging from their tents and gathering up gear. There was a solemnity to these proceedings: part of the experience is the challenge of poor weather, and much of the gear is designed with that in mind. The cloud thickened to drizzle, making eagle-watching pointless, but we still decided to continue to Lough Currane.

We drove through Waterville, then turned left towards Lough Currane, and parked just before the first lake inlet. The map shows a road running along the shore of the lake, but there was a surprising amount of woodland along the northern stretch of lakeshore, so views of the water were intermittent. Streams were running off the mountains towards the lake, and made gurgling, splashing, flowing noises among ferns, flowers and other vegetation. Instead of being a walk by a lake, this was a stroll through the vegetable kingdom, a kind of Victorian palimpsest of detail, rigour and natural purity. I rehearsed fragments of that lore, gleaned over the years: royal and buckler fern, bracken, herb robert, meadow sweet, wall pennywort, purple loosestrife, great wood rush, tufted vetch, yellow stonecrop, cow wheat, self heal, tutsan, honeysuckle, montbretia. There were many other plants along the roadside or in the mixed woodland of grey willow, holly, hazel, rowan, alder, oak and ash. Praeger's ghost walked with me as I mused on rarities I may never learn. A phrase of Praeger's repeated itself in my mind: the Irish flora is still an unworked field. Two years earlier, for example, my friends Chris and Lynda Huxley found an extensive new station for spring gentian on the shore of Lough Carra close to a well-known site.

One of the streams running to the lake fell over a vertical rock face about seven metres high. Following a recent squall, water was streaming off the lip at the top like a miniature Cascade de la Pissevache ('cow-piss cascade'), an Alpine waterfall that I saw in a painting in Geneva years ago.[39] To either side of the stream, a richly hued green moss with a deep pile covered the rock. On one side, the stream ran into the moss and then re-emerged from the tips of the moss as glistening, green-tinted teardrops.

I felt that there was little hope of an eagle that day, even if we were walking in superb eagle country. Lough Currane is richly stocked with salmon and sea trout, as witness the traffic of cormorants up and down the lake. Mullach Beg, the mountain to the south rises in an impressive escarpment to over 300 metres, and the upper section of the lake has many reefs, outcrops and islands. To the south-east, behind Mullach Beg, Eagle's Hill rises to 542 metres, overlooking the Kerry Way. Away to the east, there is a splendid series of peaks, lakes and cliffs holding great prospects for the species, but the scale of it all made it unlikely that we would spot anything on one casual visit.

After the walk we drove to the end of the lake; on the way, one large bird in the sky disappeared after a moment over the mountain before I could get the binoculars into my hands. This would be our only allowance from Lough Currane that morning. Finally we met an angler, who had not seen an eagle that year, despite many days out on the lake. He boasted in a pleasant way about some very large sea trout he had caught, and I indulged him by listening, and saying how famous Lough Currane was for their size.

In the afternoon, we bathed at Ballinskelligs beach, another great theatre of childhood: one toddler in a pink swimsuit and bonnet ran ahead of her siblings along the waves, heading into a great adventure, and was not hampered by a fussing parent, until she fell on her face, picked herself up, and returned to the others unscathed.

Kenmare
July 18

After five hours of hard rain overnight I lay listening to curlew, ringed plover and other shorebirds through gaps in the hammering noise of heavy raindrops. In the morning we walked about the campsite in a daze at first, the world slow to come round and get the noise of rain out of its head. I got a text message from a friend telling me that the young swifts in Castlebar were ready to fledge.

Jessica and I agreed that we would head home, if not by the most direct route. The heavy rain had put water in the streams and rivers, and I was interested in seeing the Cascade de la Pissevache again. (Our term for such trips is a 'rain safari', when streams and rivers are in spate following heavy rain.) Going down to Lough Currane would also give us a chance, perhaps the last on this trip, of seeing an eagle.

We stopped at Derrynane House, Daniel O'Connell's ancestral home in a wild setting at the south-western tip of the Iveragh Peninsula. I had been told of another eagle name near here: *Clochán an Fhiolair* ('stony place of the eagle'). The map shows a stony hill near the sea called Eagle Hill, just south of the house. Like Cregganilra on Killary Harbour, this modest hill would not have been suitable for a nest site, but was clearly used as a landing point and feeding spot with a good view of the surrounding district.

The gardens at Derrynane, with huge gunnera, bamboo, palm and cypress trees and antique camellias, are now in the care of the state. O'Connell's memory is preserved in an almost Georgian setting of fine furniture, a library and the hunting grounds of the estate. His dislike of republicanism puts him beside Edmund Burke, that other great constitutionalist. An annexe also houses the Roman-style chariot that was made for O'Connell after his release from prison. This Roman aspiration makes him look like a Napoleon of the Catholic cause.

The library at Derrynane House contains books from the Liberator's time and some that were acquired by his descendants. It shows that the family was well educated, with an interest in European literature: Schiller found a place on the shelves here alongside Tom Moore and Walter Scott. The scene is a paradigm of the moment in Lady Morgan's *The Wild Irish Girl* when the English hero Horatio comes into the heroine's boudoir in her house in the remote west of Ireland. Up to that moment Horatio imagined that Glorvina, the wild Irish girl, was a kind of Wordsworthian Lucy, living far away from decadent society. Confounding all his preconceptions, he discovers that this innocent child of Irish nature is immersed in the sentimental literature of the eighteenth century, and her room is furnished with current periodicals from London and Paris. He has gone to the outermost extreme of Gaelic remoteness to find a cornucopia of worldly belles-lettres. Even in the sixteenth century, it was reported that John Harington's translation of Ariosto's *Orlando Furioso* had some fashionable success among the ladies of Galway. Still, the notion persists that because a place is remote, its people are somehow uncultured. This idea never occurred to Wordsworth and his collaborators when they were based in Somerset and Cumbria. It had some currency in Ireland in the fifties and sixties of the twentieth century and must have derived from the bias of a few snobs among the Dublin press. Some writers such as Patrick Kavanagh were seriously distracted by this prejudice.

The lady at the desk spoke proudly of the renovations that had just been completed, and she told us about the history of the house in the care of the state. The state has also protected a stretch of coastal machair within the grounds and in the absence of grazing animals it was packed with flowers: lady's bedstraw, eyebright, clover, and lots of pyramidal orchids in a vivid shade of magenta.

On the way to Kenmare there were many cataracts falling into coums and the heads of high valleys. The name *Coum na nEasaigh* ('coum of the waterfalls') made perfect sense that day, with a spread of cataracts streaming into the coum from the mountain above.

We set out for home the following day, having spent almost two weeks in eagle country outside Mayo. We had been told of twelve pairs established in Ireland, and of that total we had seen five birds, plus the eaglet at Mountshannon. I was also taking home with me a rumour of a sea-eagle pair established somewhere on Achill.

Kenmare – Westport
July 19

I slept for nine hours and woke to a pleasant ache and weariness in my legs. After several nights in a sleeping bag on a hard surface, fresh sheets and a mattress were a special pleasure, as they were to Pádraig Ó Conaire after days on the road with the little black donkey, his *asal beag dubh*.

We stopped at Knockbrack, outside Abbeyfeale, to heat up soup for lunch and I told Jessica about the holidays I spent there at Auntie May's place. I was obsessed with fishing the river and knew every run and pool of that little stream. It was the place where I really got to know the feel of the countryside. When I read Heaney, his countryside is my countryside, much of it based on my memories of Auntie May's house at Knockbrack.

I heard sand martins, and I remembered them breeding in a clay riverbank at the nearby landfill site. The pool of the river running past our lunch spot was not pretty-looking after all the dry weather, but it held salmon parr: they made ripples and were rising to the surface.

On our drive out from Abbeyfeale, we passed a woman in lycra leggings and a pink singlet, out for exercise along the road. She was about my own age, and exemplified the vitality and self-confidence of this era and this season. I wondered whether she was among the group of small kids whom I used to see swimming in the river.

Later in the afternoon we found that everything at Thoor Ballylee, Yeats's house outside Gort, was closed owing to flooding. Silt stains on doors and walls to waist height marked winter water levels, but the woods and streams were glorious, and we watched a grey wagtail family on the river. One juvenile with a shorter tail was calling for food from one of the adults. We brewed tea, with a goldcrest family in the trees around us, a treecreeper on a tree trunk overhead, and a mallard family on the river. I thought it a pity that there was no writer's residency there, nothing to connect the place with living literature, only a museum, and that one shut. At the same time, nowhere was more alive than that river and those woods.

Belderg
July 29

Belderg has a special place in north Mayo sea-eagle lore because the ornithologist Robert Warren visited there in 1892 and interviewed one of the old cliffmen, Martin McAndrew. McAndrew was '70 years of age and still as enthusiastic about cliff-climbing as ever and full of stories of the eagles and eggs he took off the cliffs.' Warren wrote to the ornithologist Richard James Ussher:

> He told us that since he robbed the eggs about three years ago they had left that part of the cliffs and had moved on to those near Porturlin … ten miles further west and for some years past only one pair frequented that part of the coast … he described the birds breeding on the cliffs as the 'Grey eagles almost as grey as a goose' and that they had white feathers in the tail. I then asked what they chiefly fix on, and he said hares, and occasionally a lamb, but that they were not nearly so destructive to lambs as the 'Black Eagle' which sometimes came down there from the mountains near Corick and Bangor where they bred.[40]

Warren knew that the old *ailleadóir* was describing both species of eagle, the 'Grey' or sea eagle and the 'Black' or golden eagle. These creatures, in the account of this old man, speak to us from an otherworld as tantalising as Yeats's supernatural figures, but with an added dimension of tragedy because we know that they were eventually completely exterminated, as none of Yeats's fairies could ever be.

By the time Jessica and I set out for Belderg, the sea eagle chick at Mountshannon was flying, and had been filmed hovering briefly over the pine trees on Cribby Island. We had set our sights on Benwee Geevraun, a hill on the coast just west of Belderg harbour, where sea eagles bred until the early 1940s. There were also two place names on the coast east of the harbour: *Scraith an Iolra* ('eagle green') and *Carraig an Iolra* ('eagle rock'), which I had in mind to see. But our plans for the day were completely thrown when we met a local man, Peter Bourke, who offered to show us the coast near his home, and the way to Benmore, which was his name for Benwee. His enthusiasm was a gift we could not refuse: we were first shown his antique Ferguson tractor from the 1940s and then we walked out across the bog as he commented on scars and trenches in the peat and their history: where a log of ancient timber had been dug up; where an attempt had been made to dig out a fox's den, leaving several metres of open trenchwork before the effort was abandoned.

As it turned out, our guide had more interest in showing us Horse Island than directing us towards Benwee, but we were glad of distraction. Horse Island is really a peninsula, with a causeway of rubble between it and the mainland. A smaller sea stack has become separated to the west, and as we stood there taking in this unexpected wonder of the Mayo coast, a foaming, turquoise sea was breaking around its base. Great black-backed gulls sat in session on its flat, grassy top.

Peter led us down the causeway to *Oileán na gCapall*. Old copper mines had been dug here into the base of the cliffs, and the ruined wall of an old mine building was set neatly into the line of the cliff, as unobtrusive as anything a modern planner could have devised, like a fantasy of survival within earshot of the sea. A fault in the geology has produced an arched tunnel through the island, about the size of a single motorway lane, with waves washing its floor. Another fault has been plugged by magma of a later eruption; the plug sits down against the flank of Horse Island like an inset column. Our guide broke copper-stained rocks to show us gleams of a mineral like fool's gold.

The gap between Horse Island and the mainland acts like a hook to catch flotsam from the west, and Peter told us proudly about the many odds and ends salvaged here over the years: a large spar of matchwood, a span of netting to protect his silage bales from the crows, bottles with messages brought by the Gulf Stream from America's east coast. That day's trove was a leather football with the Premier League logo.

We scrambled across rubble and climbed up onto the flat grassy top of Horse Island: a tight sward of thrift, and some blooms of cross-leaved heath in more sheltered hollows. I mentioned eagles at Benwee to the west, and he instantly pointed south to another Benmore, five kilometres south of Belderg. This is a hill I climbed in the late 1990s, with no thought of eagles or their history. When I came back to the car that day, I was invited for tea and apple tart by a farmer and his wife, who told me I had just been to Eagle Rock. They did not ask me for my name, and I did not ask for theirs.

'That's called the Eagle's Nest,' said Peter, referring to the same escarpment. When we talked about the reintroduction programmes, he was quick to mention the threat to lambs, which I countered by saying that the Irish Farmers' Association in Donegal supported the golden eagle programme, and that sea eagles were no threat, citing Norwegian experience.

Benwee Geevraun has a rusty-coloured eroding face of

cliff on its inner, eastern side, beside a very steep outer slope or *strapa*, which is the local word for a grassy ledge. Sheep are drawn to these pockets of undisturbed growth, where the farmer sometimes has to go down on a rope to get back a trapped animal. At the foot of the eroding cliff is a place called *Poll na Binne*, ('the hollow of the peak'). In October 1997, a German and three others got wrecked in a narrow cove here when their currach was swamped in heavy conditions. Both the German, Will Ernst von Below, and a local rescue diver, Michael Heffernan, died; the others were saved. Thus any talk of eagles in this place (they bred here before 1907) has been displaced by a recent human tragedy of two lives lost despite individual heroism and a large rescue effort.

There have been other human tragedies along this coast, anonymous ones which Peter broached by saying that he likes to keep his gates closed to deter people from coming here to commit suicide, as they do at Céide. A memorial mass is held there every year nowadays, to commemorate those lives lost. We crept forward to a sheer cliff edge on the outer rim of Horse Island and looked down at rocks twenty metres below, our thoughts only of wonder, and manageable dangers.

As we came round the eastern rim of the island, a ringed plover fledgling ran out from under Jessica's foot; another appeared in front of us. We approached slowly and discovered it lying flat on a pale-coloured rock, perfectly camouflaged on the lichen. Our host was delighted and declared that he had never seen such a thing before, in all his years coming here. We were delighted too at such a frail little thing having the means to outwit the patrolling great black-backed gulls.

Horse Island, and the adjoining coast, had been a play- and

trove-ground for Peter since childhood. He talked about risks and challenges, thrills and spills, for him and his companions on these rocks. Despite being told by their parents not to take risks, they naturally did; and the worst thing they could do was, not to get knocks or bruises, but to tear their clothes, as clothes were expensive in those days. I thought of children in overcrowded estates in cities, where the same impulses of challenge and daring mean that kids get into trouble with the law, and are accused of anti-social behaviour. The same generation is being shepherded away from risk into controlled environments and will have few memories of direct encounters with the power of the elements, such as you get at places like Horse Island, in a great theatre of light, sea and stone.

At the eastern end of Horse Island, a geological fault has resulted in a deep, perfectly straight fissure, not much more than a metre wide, cutting north–south through almost the entire width of the island, and almost creating a separate sea stack. We walked around this twenty-metre-deep gap in the ground with the sea surging underneath. Peter walked fifty metres back and showed us how he jumped the gap. Even the man in his fifties had not lost the daredevil spirit of youth.

On our way back to the mainland, we scrambled down to a tunnel at the foot of Horse Island where Peter pointed out a vault, like a flooded arcade, with a large opening to the sea at the back. A lopsided rectangle of light shimmered above a cobbled floor; seawater washed the rocks at our feet with what Keats called 'shadowy sound'. A wide, sloping surface of rock stretches across this open-ended cave, about the same area, and as steep, as the seating in a small cinema. Our host, who must have peered into this cave thousands of times, suggested the comparison.

This stretch of coast is, in most public senses, unrecorded, or at least under-recorded. Apart from a few scholarly excursions such as compilations of place names and folklore, there has been no publicity surrounding Horse Island. The emergency services appeared there a few years ago as they attempted to save lives, but since then this place has been the preserve of Peter Bourke and his guests. In another context, Horse Island could be the focus of birdwatching, abseiling, angling, landscape painting and hillwalking. There would be a tea shop selling souvenirs and watercolours, and a museum of industrial archaeology based around the theme of copper mining. The causeway would be secured with a railing, and signs everywhere would warn of the dangers of going too close to the cliff edge. The whole place would be marketed and branded out of existence, so that the socially shy visitor like myself would yearn to go farther, or come back on a quiet day off-season, when the tea shop and museum would be shut, in order to experience something authentic, without the product packaging.

We said a grateful farewell after a tour of this proud countryman's property. Benwee headland would be unvisited that day; instead, we drove to the small road past Glinsk towards Srahataggle and Porturlin, marvelling at the bleak grandeur of the area. I pointed out Pollagh, where I had camped a month earlier and heard the calls of Manx shearwater in the small hours. At Porturlin, we watched a man launch a one-man currach, a cockboat to get him to a trawler moored in the bay.

On the way home, I went for a brief swim at Mulranny; Jessica sat and watched me jumping about for a few minutes in the choppy waves at high tide.

Achill Island

August 4

I eventually got away to Achill on the August bank holiday Monday. I knew that the report of sea eagles on Achill might be a deliberate fiction designed to waste people's time. If there were eagles on Achill, the fact had not come to the attention of the local papers, and they would certainly have made a fuss about it, trumpeting the return of eagles to Achill after almost a hundred years. Eagles have a strong place in local memory: the myth persists that 'the last eagle in Ireland' was killed here, and locals will tell you that Achill means 'eagle', although the connection is apparently groundless, and is based merely on a similarity between the Latin *Aquila* and the island's name.

If there were sea eagles on Achill, I thought they might be hiding at the western end of the island, among the cliffs and corrie lakes of Croaghaun. No eagle wheeling off the cliffs at Menawn in the south, or off Slievemore in the north, could go unnoticed during the busy tourist season. Nonetheless, in the interests of a duty I think of as science, I felt obliged to check the woodland around Sraheens Lough just outside Achill Sound. There are splendid old Scots pines here growing out of a flood of rhododendron which will eventually kill them. A few years ago, a group of us took what we hoped would be a short cut off the mountain through undergrowth here and ended up in a fifteen-foot-deep tangle of rhododendron. The barrier of horizontal branches blocking our way almost defeated us; a combination of crawling, limbo dancing and high-branch balancing eventually got us back to the road, exhausted and flush with new rhododendron knowledge. This plant would be a powerful security barrier under an eagle nest site, and this woodland had always looked to me like a possible spot in the east of Achill.

The rain had already passed when I turned off the main road out of Achill Sound and followed a bog track for a few hundred metres. I turned the car to face back east, giving me a view of the lake, and the Corraun and Nephin Beg mountains. A large curtain of flood-bearing rain had veiled the Owenduff catchment, and I felt an undercurrent of excitement at the prospect of swollen rivers bringing sea trout up from the sea.

The bog was strikingly quiet in August. Six weeks earlier these moors had been busy with skylarks and pipits, but their broods had fledged, and the cuckoos that preyed on them had gone back to Africa. I heard brief bird calls and watched dark butterflies rising and falling in a hurried flare of desire off the bog, but the crowded territories of song had shut down for another year. Banks of cloud were stacked high above the mountain massif of Corraun, like the cloud in Paul Henry's paintings, and I watched this canvas through the early afternoon, searching for a speck in the high distance. Any that did materialise were large gulls moving between the lake and the sea, and one raven pair. These birds strolled about casually: nothing in their behaviour suggested an enemy or rival in the trees.

Straight ahead of me in the distance, about eight kilometres away, were the scree falls east of Lough Cullylea on Corraun, which I had surveyed from the top of the plateau nine weeks earlier. One stretch of pale-grey scree under the escarpment was shaped like a human figure with raised arms, as if this person had just jumped from the mountaintop above. I think of this hillside scree figure as another appearance of Dáithí Bán, the Erris giant whose fortress was the cairn on the top of Corslieve.

After a vigil of two hours I decided that there were no eagles on this side of Achill, and I persuaded myself that if there were any here, they would have been noticed at Rock House, a hunting and fishing lodge to the north of Corraun, whose owners are alert to such things. With no reports of eagles from the eastern side of Achill, that left the dramatic stretch of coast at the north-western end of the island, around Croaghaun mountain and Saddle Head.

My observations up to that point were: a hillside giant, a few birds and butterflies, some clouds – there would have been more if I had had patience. The truth is, with a fly rod in the car, I wanted to be off in pursuit of sea trout, and I made a pretence at science as an excuse for moving on. Alternatively, it might have been more valuable to cultivate a Buddha-like state of non-attachment to any knowledge, and instead sit there with an open mind, emptied of all pretence. As Krapp might have said, in Samuel Beckett's play, 'Go off fishing, you bastard, and get on with this drivel in the morning!'

Following his advice, I explored two lakes that lay at the

north-eastern tip of Achill, but neither of them had the direct stream to the sea that I was hoping for. The larger one, Dooniver, is a saline lagoon, with a wild sandbar separating it from Blacksod Bay, and I walked along part of it, raising redshanks and curlews as I went, measuring space by wader calls, rather as a sheep farmer controls a hillside with his dog. I made for a ruined house on the sandbar, with a gull's nest of bleached and withered kelp rods atop a ruined gable. Other rods fallen from the pile littered the concrete floor, each of them as variable in their consistency as the marks on a Jackson Pollock drip picture. On the way back, I picked a large, perfectly white sea-snail shell from the shingle and remembered that at Mountshannon Daniel had asked for one like this so that he could listen to the sea. I held it to my ear to check for the distant noise of hissing surf, and kept it for him.

Later, I sat overlooking Lough Doo, the smaller of the two: a freshwater lake with its sentries of herons and citizenry of mallard. The great pyramid of Slievemore rose beyond it, and much farther out, like a punctuation mark on the horizon, was Black Rock with its lighthouse, where a coastguard helicopter crashed in March 2017, killing all four of its crew. A flare of evening light from the sun behind Slievemore lay on the rim of the sea, and this remote rock was floating on the glare, like a citadel, innocent of the heroic drama that was to unfold here two and a half years later, in atrocious weather, as they searched for the lost helicopter and its crew.

Then, a rising greyness thickened in the south over Corraun and dissolved the forms that had just kept the imagination entertained. Perspectives shortened in the rain:

a woman passed with a wheelbarrow full of garden cuttings; another went by with a dog on a lead. Life reverted to the small geography of fields and farmyards. My grand designs had to be postponed.

Writing these reflections had cost me an opportunity to pitch the tent while the evening was still dry. Now the rain looked as though it had set in for the night and I would have to spend several minutes getting wet as I fumbled with guy ropes and rods before the tent was secure.

Just as I thought the rain would clear, it came on again in a stronger wave.

Eventually, during a lull I stepped out of the car into a cloud of midges. I retreated, drove a little way to a disused quarry, and got the tent out, but after a couple of minutes of torment on that sultry August evening I gave up and beat a retreat to a B & B.

Dooagh
August 5

Thick cottonwool cloud was low over Croaghaun; not even the grand corrie at Acorrymore was visible. The wind was enough to keep the midges down, but there seemed little point in attempting a walk to Saddle Head that morning. Navigation would be tricky, and any mythical or real creatures would be wrapped in fog.

Achill is where my parents had their first holiday together as a married couple, in 1956, just before I was born. There was an eggcup marked 'Achill' on a shelf at home, one of a collection that they began at that time. Heinrich Böll was a visitor to Achill in those days, and he has left visual and literary records of its earthy charms, so I can visualise the place my parents visited, while they were still London residents, from Böll's 1962 film, *Irland und seine Kinder*, with its donkeys, shawled women and turf creels. Maybe it was while walking on Achill, in the fresh air of the Atlantic, that my mother and father took the decision to leave smog-filled London and come back to Ireland to raise their family.

That morning I felt memory pursuing its almost ineluctable claims: even if the day had been clear and I were striding up Croaghaun on my way out to Saddle Head, their ghosts would still have been on the beach at Keel, waiting for their as-yet-unborn son to get back home safely.

Croaghaun
August 9

The morning's weather appeared to be holding, and I was driving back to Achill to see if Croaghaun was free of clouds. Coming out along Corraun I got my first preview of the mountain: the whole spine was visible beyond the other ridges and peaks of the island. This was Paul Henry's early morning time, when few people are stirring and a milkiness softens the surfaces and colours of distant slopes: on the way into Achill Sound, the northern face of Clare Island presented that full, abstract pyramid of mountain that Henry loved; in the foreground there were small-scale houses on the south-eastern coast of Achill on a low slope above the

Sound. This was the first of several canvases that assembled themselves. As I drove across the island, alternations of cloud cover and sunlight meant that lower ridges near Cashel were in dark shadow, giving the bog an air of menace, while the peak of Slievemore soared in bright sunlight. The mountain was a rugged forehead, purplish in those conditions.

At Keem Bay, under Croaghaun, I parked near three motor homes. Registration plates from Italy and France gave this place a prospect looking eastwards not just on Mayo, but on Europe, and even on life itself, a point from which a whole philosophy could develop. For now, though, the philosophers were still asleep.

I traced an ambitious route in pencil, running along the headland as far as Achill Head, then turning east to climb the twin peaks of Croaghaun; my pencil ran on after that to Saddle Head and turned back as far as Annagh to visit a series of lakes perched above the sea, before finally crossing the saddle back to the bog track that leads to Dooagh village. This would be a true pilgrim's or hero's performance in a day, beyond my comfort zone, so I abridged what Praeger called 'one of the most exhilarating walks in Ireland.'[41]

I attacked the eastern peak of Croaghaun directly by crossing the road and taking my first steps up a grassy ramp which the sheep use. It felt good to be into the ascent so quickly and conveniently. Within a couple of minutes, a chough was calling below me, announcing the start of the day, and more of these squealing calls encouraged me on. The first time I took out the notebook, midges crowded on my writing hands, so I kept moving, if slowly, like a sheep pottering about in its own thoughts, rather than a conqueror with a single purpose: to climb.

At 200 metres I was walking among tent-sized boulders, conglomerates studded with quartz pebbles from ancient depositions, and I heard, for the first time, the sound of running water a couple of metres underground. There were two ridges above me, the further one softened by hazy distance. On the western side, above Keem Bay, at the lowest point of the ridge running back from Moyteoge Head, a tiny pool of sea was just starting to fill as I went higher; this is the horizon I would lift as I climbed. In a short time, Inishbofin had risen above the watchtower on the headland, to float on the distant sea.

Deer sedge (*Trichophorum cespitosum*) was turning russet, the colour that transforms whole hillsides in October, and at 300 metres, on an exposed part of the ridge, there was that ginger-coloured moss that I associate with true upland. As I rested near a boulder, I saw a grasshopper and caught it in my fist; after a few attempts to escape, it calmed down and settled on my forefinger, perhaps dazed and defeated by its predator, or just enjoying the smell of sun lotion after our lovers' struggle. Its back was grass-blade green, tapering to a point; the upper back had a plate the shape of a lady's sleeveless dress: a central, vertical yellow stripe with vivid neon green on either side, and black outer bands. So I made design notes for Christopher Kane, but a midge pinched my hand as a signal to move on. I had to provoke the grasshopper to jump off my finger, back to its kingdom in the heather.

I looked south again to see the first shower of rain coming over the sea like the landing beams of an alien spacecraft. Keem Bay had diminished to a sliver of turquoise under the mountain. As I turned north towards the summit and entered the scree field, Slievemore had a cloud top like a smoking volcano, and there were archipelagoes of shadow on the glittering sea. It had taken two hours' walking for my spirits and limbs to wake up, among the hazardous, jumbled steps of grey scree. Every few paces, a new perspective opened up: the steep coast at the back of Slievemore, on Blacksod Bay, with a fringe of lace at the rocks' base. A currach was heading out to sea from Keem beach, the size of a midge to the naked eye.

Approaching the summit at 688 metres, any calculation seems redundant, superfluous. You abandon the checks of perspective, you have no interest in looking back, everything is pitched upwards and forwards: you pass a modest cairn and then, gingerly, come to the edge, afraid lest space might swallow you. The Matterhorn-style point of Croaghaun had now appeared several hundred metres away to the left; over three kilometres beyond that, with a slight milk veil of distance, the axe-head scramble to Achill Head. I was standing on *Tóin a' Chruacháin*, 'the arse of Croaghaun', and a fine arse it was. The slope to the sea here is not quite perpendicular, but if you slipped there would be nothing to stop you walloping and sliding down for some 600 metres. Rock strata on this northern face are stacked like untidy dinner plates; scree falls under here must go all the way into the sea itself.

The inquisitive Canon Otway had his moment of greatest exhilaration here, having climbed to this point from the east. His sublime exclamation, in *A Tour of Connaught* (1839), is a fine example of the high Romantic mood, complete with full religious implication; the occasion was focussed by the sighting of a sea eagle. 'In such a place,' he wrote, 'and in an island that gets its name from eagles, it would be disgraceful

to the "genius loci" if he would not show us an eagle or two.'
His wish was granted:

> The observation was scarcely made, when upward, from
> a ledge of rock beneath our feet, sprung a noble bird, and
> we could see him open his beak and shiver his feathers,
> just as a wild beast would stretch himself when rising from
> his lair; and then he soared directly over our heads, took
> a wheel round, as much as to say, I don't understand what
> these fellows want here, and, keeping close to the stratum
> of clouds that was still incumbent on the topmost cliff, he
> kept afloat exactly under it, as if coasting along a ceiling,
> and then struck away northwards, taking his direction
> towards the highlands of Inniskea.

His description of this bird in the wild setting of north-
west Achill gave way to the following meditation:

> The look-out to ocean was sublime. Oh! What would I
> not give to stand here, if possible, and witness a tempest
> from the west; but even as I did see it, it was elevating to
> the mind, – filling you with grand conceptions of God's
> creation, and raising your imagination to consider what
> the mind may yet take in, when escaped from this mortal
> coil; and the untramelled intellect can see, understand,
> and more intensely adore the God of the ocean and the
> mountain – the God of power, and oh! thanks be to Jesus,
> the pardoning God of love.[42]

Otway's style, and the genre of travel writing generally at this
time, allowed a writer to combine effusions of this kind with
more sober descriptions of geology, antiquities and folklore.
Otway deserves to be celebrated alongside the better-known
W. H. Maxwell for the range of his interests and speculations,

and the rich detail of his accounts of Mayo and the west.

On the occasion of his visit to Achill, Otway recorded another memorable piece of eagle lore from Mayo tradition, with a link to the Bills Rocks, twelve kilometres to the south of Croaghaun. It concerns a legendary ancestor of the Marquess of Sligo (Lord Altamont of Westport House), who gave offence to a Catholic friar, and, like the pagan Sweeney, was cursed by the priest to haunt the Bills after his death in the form of a sea eagle. Here he stayed for years, 'proud and melancholy, like Lord Altamont, only in feathered instead of robed magnificence'. This tradition of the soul of a Marquess of Sligo haunting the Bills Rocks is corroborated by the naturalist William Thompson, who mentions an eagle on the Bills being called 'Old Brown' by the locals – Brown being the family surname of the Marquess.[43]

The story related by Otway gets a strong political flavour when Catholic Emancipation was granted, with one of the Marquess's descendents at Westport House, Howe Peter, voting for the measure, 'perhaps to disenchant his progenitor. On the day on which the noble marquess said in his place in the House of Lords, CONTENT, up flew the eagle from the Billies … soaring until he pierced the clouds, and entered the empyrean.' The tale gets a final twist, however, with an added element borrowed from the story of St Patrick banishing snakes from Ireland. The eagle does not manage to ascend fully to heaven; the soul of the old Marquess will only be granted release from this world when 'mass is said in Westport House, and the black slugs are driven out of Ireland.'[44] The story reflects the religious divisions on Achill at the time, with Otway's party from the Doogort Mission being jeered by hostile locals as they passed through the villages of Dooagh and Keem.

A faint track along the edge of the ridge took me down slowly and steadily. The biggest seabirds moving across the surface below were only specks, even in binoculars; but then a great black-backed gull appeared on the updraught, being lifted vertically above the face and not needing a single wingbeat to move along the face of the mountain. The commotion of waves at the shore was refined at that distance to an even hum, like the drone of a busy motorway.

A kilometre east of Tonacroaghaun, the coast starts to curve out to Saddle Head, and the crook of that curve holds a beach that must be formed of many scree boulders off the mountain, sifted and shaped by hundreds of years of wave action. The binoculars found a group of seals ashore on these boulders, like a cluster of quotation marks at that range, and more were hanging in the white foam of the massive breakers.

Then, scanning the ridge above this seal beach, I saw an eyrie site and my attention fixed on it like a military instrument at the moment of an air strike. A jumble of cliffs appeared, as if someone had carelessly stacked three-, four-, and five-storey sections of bare blocks of rock on a ledge under the ridge line, and where two of these leaned against each other, there was a sheltered opening, with a broad frontage, and another precipitous fall down to the seal beach. There are many other inaccessible ledges on this north-west corner of Achill, but I celebrated this above all other options, on behalf of Achill's eagles, past and future. This entire section of coast, between Achill Head and Slievemore, is certainly vast and remote enough to harbour a rumour of sea eagles, one that could hold good for several sceptical visits before being laid to rest. No eagles would appear that day, even though visibility and conditions were ideal.

The ridge line divided briefly into two, with a roofless railway tunnel between two narrow spurs: the right-hand one looked safer, and gave me a new perspective above Lough Bunnafreeva West, the first lake in this north-facing series – according to Praeger, 'a place so lonely and sterile and primeval that one might expect to see the *péist* or other Irish water-monster rising from the inky depths of the tarn.'[45] The lakewater was an intense, pure lambency of freshwater, of no stable colour, and not dark, with a collar of grey stones all around. It lies at just over 300 metres; that's 200 metres lower than the ridge that I stood on to take a photograph. Great black-backs were congregated on the shore while a few of them shuffled their wings in this pure water. Eventually, one of the adults was hoisted up to my level on an updraught, and began to shout my presence to the lonely coum. I was intrigued by the trails that skirted this lake: one along the western shore cut across the scree and appeared to divide it. Could human hands have cleared boulders here to create the path? For what purpose?

On the far side of the lake, on a moraine that dams the corrie, a white pyramid of quartz the size of a tent caught my eye among other large boulders. When I moved on, I spotted another of these fairy stones, this one a block as big as a bale of silage, marking its fall from the mountain. Scars and stone patterns on the open ground stretched for a couple of kilometres all the way to Saddle Head. My amazement at this place deepened a little way farther on, when two more lakes came into view: Lough Nakeeroge and Lough Bunnafreeva East. A little glen was formed where water drained into Lough Nakeeroge and there, in the bracken, was the unmistakeable pattern of lazy beds. Above this glen, on a raised slope with its back to the sea, was the outline of fields which someone thought of winning from a hill undercut by the ocean. Human husbandry in such a setting is a miracle; my credulity could stretch to this only as a summer site, where people grew potatoes and herded cattle until autumn storms drove them and their livestock home. A large igloo-shaped boulder nearby appeared like a stone habitation, its surface formed into curious sections, as if constructed – but no, I dismissed my brief fantasy of eskimo life at the back of Croaghaun. It was only a large boulder.

The last lake in this series is at Annagh. It comes into view only at the last moment, when the spur off the mountain suddenly falls away steeply. The dark slate of this long, narrow lake is only a few metres above sea level, but the contrast is dramatic between its inert waters and the foaming, turquoise sea breaking onto a grey beach at the outer rim of the boulder bar. I thought about going down to swim in that effervescence and stored up the dream for another day. Instead of dropping down to Annagh, I turned south, and headed for the bog track taking me back to Dooagh.

I had seen no one on Croaghaun, and very few recent boot marks, but then a couple appeared on the ridge 400 metres away. The woman was rolling up a ground mat which they had been using, perhaps for some yogic meditation, midges permitting (there was a holistic festival in Achill that weekend). They moved away to the south, towards the bog track I was headed for, and drew me down in their direction. The grass was deep on the sheltered slope and had grown over the sheep trail I was following. My feet swished through long grasses and lichens; they sifted my purpose out of all these shifting stalks, and my boots crunched on the sedges of late summer growth. I paused to listen to the wind moving over this unmarked ground and heard a sibilance everywhere. The land was singing.

In Dooagh I was back – or was it forward? – in a different time. SUVs were parked all over the village beside holiday homes and summer lets. An opulence sat at kitchen tables or on sheltered balconies, contemplating an unsteady idea of escape, extremity or simplicity, which I could not inhabit.

I rang from Gielty's Bar and Restaurant for a taxi and got impatient when the driver took longer than the half hour he said. After an hour and ten minutes I rang again: he had been waiting for me at Gielty's and had not seen me; perplexed by this, I told him I was still there, and had seen no one. He would be there in five minutes, he said, and explained that he was in a white minibus. Eventually, a white minibus appeared, I hailed it, but the driver saluted back and drove past. Enter, into this local drama, the painter Camille Souter, who must have heard of my plight, and who told me that Gielty's, in local reference, is not the shop I was standing in front of, but Gielty's pub farther up the street. By then, after an hour and twenty minutes' waiting, I had given up and set out on foot for Keem. Five minutes later, as I passed a cheerful house with colourful flowers, a lady hailed me and asked if I was looking for a taxi. I said I was, and that I had been waiting at the shop. She told me again that for them, Gielty's was the pub; the shop was known simply as 'the shop'. Her husband appeared, somewhat abashed, and drove me to Keem. On the way there, he mentioned that people ring for taxis from the pub and do not bother to come out into the street to wait. I brushed aside his apology by saying, 'That's travel,' and we left it at that.

Fahy
August 10

I had been restless in bed all night, bathed in sweat under the duvet, as if my body would not shut down after the exertions of the day and was still working through impressions. Then I lay on the chaise longue, in sunlight, feeling a pleasant ache in my ankles from all the steps taken on Croaghaun's stones and boulders. I dozed for a while, then noticed the sky clouding over, and wind stirring in the tops of the osiers outside the window. The weather forecast mentioned an early autumn storm, the aftermath of Hurricane Bertha whipping these islands, and as the stirring of leaves increased to a commotion, there was a sense that summer was ending.

Srahduggan
August 14

I was sitting in the Blue Lodge of the Rock House Fishery on the Owenduff, drinking tea with my friend Chris Huxley.

We had been fishing for salmon all morning without any success. The window of the lodge framed a view onto the mountains, looking directly at the jagged edge of the ridge at Coscéim, which Fergal and I crossed two months earlier. I had sat in the Blue Lodge on several occasions without ever noticing that ridge, but I was attentive to it then, because I had been up there.

The previous day, I met John Booth, one of the old herdsmen at Srahduggan in the catchment of the Owenduff. We were chatting about various things: place names, salmon, the work of the old herders, and so on. I asked him if he had seen eagles and he said no, but he remembered a time some years ago when an eagle frequented the area. The wildlife people were following it, he said, and then it was found poisoned at Srahmore, on the far side of the mountains. His story probably referred to the sea eagle from Kerry that was found dead in May 2012 near Beltra Lough, and which I had seen at Srahmore the previous autumn.

John had spent three hours on the mountain that morning, turning his cattle back from an area of bog with treacherous locháns under Corry Lough. His names for features of the area are not always the same as those on the OS map. Corry Lough he calls Corranabinna, which is the OS name for the lake to the east. Lurgandarragh is his name for the mountain with the prominent brow overlooking Srahduggan. He pointed out several blocks of quartz, which litter the right-hand slope under that summit. People pick them up, he said, and take them home as souvenirs of their walk. He created a narrative of tourism at a place that I have never visited and where I have never seen any walkers.

John is one of a declining race of men who still carry on a pastoral way of life along the rivers and on the bogs of north Mayo. Their work following cattle along these river margins and across the bogs, connects them with some of the very earliest settlers in Mayo, including Iron Age people, whose cattle-based tradition was the background to the *Táin*, the greatest story of the Heroic Age in Ireland.

He complained of soreness and stiffness in his limbs; he took the weight off his feet when we met by kneeling down on the ground, using the waterproofs he was carrying as a knee rest; it is doubtful that there will be anyone to follow this lifestyle when his time passes.

Later that afternoon, as I was leaving Srahduggan, I stopped the car to take a look at *Coire an Aifrinn* ('corrie of the mass') to the west of Coscéim, which I had seen on the day of my walk with Fergal on Bloomsday. Tatters of low cloud were being blown across the corrie wall, making observation difficult, but it did not take me long to decide that this cliff was unpromising, on a small scale compared to the much finer sites on Corraun, Achill and the north Mayo coast.

Saddle Head
August 17

I needed a scientist's determination to get me motivated for a walk to Saddle Head, following a low trail along the coast. Late summer had brought out a lot of colour on the road to Achill: orange montbretia, purple loosestrife, bell heather.

At Tonragee, between Mulranny and Achill, the smell of turf smoke suddenly suffused the car, like incense in a ritual announcing that a threshold had been crossed. Sky and air were washed after overnight rain, and a stiff north-westerly had the Mayo flags stretched tight. Clouds were pulled out of shape and smudged, without those towering heaps of ice cream I had seen a week earlier; new arrangements of light and shadow were on the land. As I drove across the island, the ridge of Menawn to my left was in full light, as was the lower ridge above Cashel, while Slievemore was a dark, abstract wedge of mountain in the distance.

Just after Bunacurry, the western end of Achill revealed itself: a sprawl of white houses behind the beach at Keel, nestled in a cradle of bog and mountain from Slievemore back to Croaghaun. This landscape is the essence of Achill, a drama of endurance in the face of the relentless, merciless Atlantic. Turf had been dried and gathered into white plastic, the orderly rows of bags on the dark bog like new tents in a refugee camp. The only eagles I saw were a large pair of bronze-painted birds in front of what used to be a Chinese restaurant at Keel during Celtic Tiger times.

I drove on to Dooagh and took the bog road I had walked on my previous visit: straight out across the grassy, unworked bog to the saddle above Annagh Strand. I picked up a light track that probably marked a fox's routine journey between mountain and lowland; it led me to a small rise packed with embroidery of Calluna, bell heather and lichens. As expected, there was an old, chalky fox turd marking this little eminence as the fox's domain. Nearby, an isolated grove of *Phragmites* reeds was waving its green banners in a hollow.

How did this plant get here?

Before I finally reached the ridge, I sat down in the lee to catch my breath: I was near the rim of a great bowl of purple moor grass and heather. The sibilance of growth was everywhere, and only once, as I tramped across, was this sound punctuated by a skylark, which rose in a spurt of notes from a song he had almost forgotten.

I floundered through deep heather for the last few hundred metres to the top. Then Lough Nakeeroge appeared at the last minute as a fine, dancing glitter of dark water close to the bottom of a steep fall. The way down was arduous, and the growth heavy, but then I saw an old drovers' trail to the east, making the same descent; I decided that that would be my way back. Farther down, as the slope bottomed out, I joined this trail, and then saw a boot print – perhaps my own from eight days earlier.

Wind off the sea was blowing hard; impressions and sights were fleeting: a kestrel, hunting across the rocky, seaward slopes, found ledges in the rush of air and moved on from niche to niche. Ravens passed. I watched for large birds gliding above the spur running from the peak of Croaghaun, and saw many large gulls riding the wind effortlessly. The trail moved out west across lower, flat ground, divided up, and was gathered in again, following the grain of sheep's passage in the direction of Saddle Head. I passed a group of ruined booley huts, tucked away on an east-facing level with a view of the steely lake and the eagle-nest crag that dominates it. Farther away, Slievemore rose unyieldingly out of a wind-torn sea. Gannets were here in number, hunting fish in the commotion of wind and water. Like white aircraft, they moved in tight circles over the water and then tilted to fold themselves into an arrowhead and fell suddenly into the sea.

The lake sits at an elevation of forty-six metres, with a narrow moraine separating it from the sea. An outflow stream makes its way through a gap in the moraine before it surrenders its fresh water to the cliffs. Some extra bit of drainage on either side of the stream has allowed half an acre of grassy pasture. I disturbed a flock of black-faced mountain sheep and walked across the tightly cropped green sward they shared with gulls. The floor was littered with gull feathers after the late summer moult, and within a few minutes two great black-backs had arrived on patrol and called to announce an intruder.

I was tempted by a swim in the lake, and made my way along a stretch of the shore looking for a convenient place to get in. When I eventually settled on a large rock sloping towards the water, I glimpsed a very large dark beetle as it sank back among the stones, having risen to the surface briefly. This was my first sight of the 'great diving beetle', *Dytiscus marginalis*, an impressive creature, which must be the origin of the place name, *Loch na Ciaróg* ('lake of the beetles'). No other beetle in this place could rival it for size or prominence. I later read that they are also capable fliers, and are guided at night by moonlight to new bodies of still water. On this occasion, a swarm of midges drove me away from a sheltered corner of Lough Nakeeroge, but not before I had solved the issue of a place name, and put a new mystery, of an aquatic night flier, in its place.

I had come as far as time allowed, and had to forgo the

last kilometre of ground that would get me to the end of Saddle Head, in favour of a more leisurely stroll back to the pass. Higher up by some 250 metres, Lough Bunnafreeva West spread its shimmering darkness among the scree and boulders, but that was a treasure stored in memory, and would not be reopened today.

Instead, I made my way to its humbler cousin, Lough Bunnafreeva East, and stopped there for a refreshing shower. The ritual of undressing, washing, then drying off and dressing again was settling to the spirit, a series of small gestures to set against the overwhelming dispersal of wild elements and spaces. There was enough of a breeze to keep off the midges, and enough shelter to keep warm the stones I was sitting on. The margins of this lake were teeming with tadpoles, and as I sat there, munching some biscuits, a tiny frog appeared on the tip of a stone just out of the water; another scaled the face of my rucksack like a free climber, failed to make it and fell back into the grass. The air was making a noise of ventilation, where a rising wind caressed grass, sedges and rocky edges on its way up the slopes. Between the lake and the top of the ridge there was a splendid series of crags and outcrops, like buttresses of the mountain: with knowledge, a walker could cross the face of this slope.

A moraine between this lake and the first Lough Nakeeroge took me back to the start of the ascent. The remote stretch of Annagh Strand was spread out to the east; I hoped that there was enough of the summer left to return there with Jessica in the next few weeks, and perhaps even splash briefly in the waves. A flotilla of great black-backs was on the lake, shuffling their wings and washing; I felt a special affinity with them as this was what I had just done myself. Once I appeared on the ridge line above them they gradually dispersed.

I picked up the rocky trail and climbed back to the top of the saddle. Ghost voices of booley people were with me as I followed their route across this tip of the island from northside pastures to southside village. Many of them were girls and women who tended cattle and milked cows here during the summer, and then regularly made the journey back to Dooagh to keep the men supplied with milk and butter. On that blustery day they were looking forward to getting back to the village and the menfolk, and their voices in my head were bright with gossip.

As it came off the top of the ridge, the trail was a shallow trench with a rough floor of stones leading to strips of old peat workings. When this faded into the grasses and sedges of the bog, it became a firm, narrow path heavily scored by sheep hooves. This was much easier going than the bumpy wading through hissing sedges of my outward journey. The path delivered me nicely onto a gravel track among the peat workings, and I made careful note of the junction: turn right off the track where there is a big flat stone in the ground just before a little stream flooding the track.

Later, in a coffee shop in Keel, I made an interesting discovery on Bob Kingston's map of Achill, framed in a hallway: the ruins above Lough Nakeeroge, which I took to be booley huts, were in fact huts used by lobster men from the Inishkeas.

Achill Head

August 30

Jessica and I met the artist John McHugh near the beach at Dooagh, returning from a walk to the point. John saw a golden eagle on Croaghaun a few years ago, and gave me more details about the observation: in the coum to the west of Lough Acorrymore, just under the ridge of Tonacroaghaun. The bird was perched about a hundred feet away from him, and then flew off to the east. It must have been one of the young eagles from the Donegal programme.

We chatted about the holidays. I told him I had not been abroad this year. 'But you've been to the Stags of Broadhaven, haven't you?' he replied.

The afternoon was clearing after a drizzly morning, just as the forecast said it would. We parked at Keem Strand and climbed to the top of the ridge. My chest felt constricted; I was unaccustomed to exercise after only two weeks of confinement, and the comings and goings of a busy house.

The glen at Keem has all the memorials and traces of Thomas Hardy's 'Unfulfilled Intentions': abandoned lazy beds and fields, ruined stone buildings, some of them of early-nineteenth-century grandeur, recalling the proselytising mission of Edmund Nangle at Doogort, on the other side of Slievemore. Set against this historical wreckage, the plants and birds have an abstract purity about them, and the sea itself, the hammering, working, shimmering sea, owes nothing to anyone. It overpowers me, as it did Ted Hughes's Crow, who tried hating the sea, but was reduced to 'a scrutty dry rabbit-dropping on the windy cliff.' Nor could Crow exist 'in the same world as the sea', because 'his lungs were not deep enough'.

That just about summed up my efforts at eagle fieldwork on Achill: the crags and cliffs had long defeated any effort at enumeration and assessment. The western slope of Croaghaun towered above us as we walked up the flank of the glen towards Achill Head; most of the mountain was visible, with only the summit hidden in streams of passing cloud. Two large boulders were conspicuous in silhouette on the steep incline approaching the top: in my gloomy mood, I searched with binoculars for Sisyphus pushing these immense burdens towards the sharp peak where they cannot settle, but will slide or roll back down. But there was no life here to satisfy such mythmaking, and we walked on.

Perspectives had changed: we could see Black Rock and its lighthouse to the north; otherwise, I was confused by a clustered series of islands and a long peninsula emerging from behind Croaghaun as the view over Blacksod Bay opened up. (The map later identified these as Duvillaun More.) The signal tower and lighthouse at Blacksod were clearly visible, but the Inishkeas were hard to pin down in these Monet-inspired landscapes, where water and clouds intermingled. A huge arc of beach east of Blacksod Point might be the sandy flats on the mainland north of Gweesalia, but how could we see them from our vantage point near Achill Head, with Croaghaun in the way? I needed a variant on the myth of Hy-Brasil, of some fabled beach, that is on no map or tourist trail, and simply tantalises the viewer with a mirage of endless sands. Canon Otway was also prompted by these bewildering vistas on Croaghaun to mention the same folklore, of a lost island appearing now and then out of the uncertain haze.

We followed a lazy, lower trail towards Achill Head, and had to climb back to the top of the cliff to get the view we were after. This involved a short scramble up a slope now in shade to 280 metres. A gull riding the updraught on the horizon was a sign that we were nearly at the clifftop. A few more paces, and we were looking out across a series of steep headlands, at the last ridge tapering away to the very end: Achill Head itself. I felt as if electrodes had been set on my chest, delivering a mild, dizzying electric shock: after a confined head-down march to reach this point, the mind suddenly had to reprogramme to a two-kilometre distance of land, set in the vastness of the Western Atlantic. We reserved for another day our plans for a scramble to the very end (where Praeger recommends nailed boots and a good head).

I said to Jessica that I believed the rumour of sea eagles established on Achill to be no more than that, a rumour. Birds the size of sea eagles should surely have turned up by now, after several visits, or we would have heard of them had they been seen. The grey Menawn cliffs rose clearly from the sea and faced in our direction: any sea eagles there would surely have been noticed by people on Keel beach. As we dropped down towards Keem Strand, I put to rest the story of sea eagles holding territory on Achill, just as summer expectations were now finished for another year.

The slope on the far side of the glen under Croaghaun had extensive patches of purple, with Calluna heather now in flower. This is the heather that truly deserves the term purple for its flowers; other heather blossoms are a kind of pink, such as bell heather, or the mauve cross-leaved heath whose flowers are now starting to fade beside the profusion of Calluna. I was very happy about this: purple never seemed like the right word for the flowers of bell heather, and as we strode home through masses of ling, flushing meadow pipits and one skylark out of their roosts in the ground cover, I felt that I had solved the mystery of Yeats's 'purple glow'.

Mweelrea

September 6

Aglorious September morning. At 7 a.m. a thick mist was spread in the hollows, with blue sky above, striped with contrails. I took the Leenane Road out of Westport. The plateau of Maumtrasna was a dark wall rising out of the morning, like a wave threatening to break over the Erriff Valley. Everything had a special clarity, as if the extra bite of cold overnight had sharpened the air, bringing things into focus. I stopped to photograph one of the plaster eagles on the gateposts at Eaglewood Lodge, and stopped again to take another photograph of Cregganilra, the eagle hillock near the mouth of the Bundorragha river. Herons and cormorants patrolled the waters at the head of Killary close to Aasleagh Falls, where sea eagles used to do the same.

Fergal was waiting at the Delphi Adventure Centre and we were on our way shortly after 9 a.m. Our path through forestry took us past climbing walls and mountain-bike circuits. A timber castle rising above the spruce trees, with rope bridges and ladders, was built as a playground for grown-ups. A few helpers were setting up ropes for health-and-safety-compliant adventures and team-building exercises. The

Adventure Centre is a busy, successful complex of apartments and facilities; Fergal worked here as a guide several years ago and knows the terrain. The stony track among the conifers soon faded out and we made our way across the bog, following a stream into the corrie under Mweelrea.

Fergal had just returned from two months' surfing in Indonesia. Our conversation turned to Islamic extremism, and I said that the West will always have a role in the Middle East to 'sort things out'; then I talked about Mountbatten's career in India, and how all hell broke loose when India and Pakistan were partitioned. I was arguing for the neo-colonial idea that, as a last resort, you rely on the Western powers as a guarantee of security in the world. Fergal countered by saying that Indonesia, a Muslim country, is also a successful democracy, and he thinks that the UN should be the arbiter in these conflicts. Our conversation dispersed on the observation that the UN is a frustrating bureaucracy, but that Ireland's peacekeeping mission with the Blue Helmets in the Golan Heights had reflected well on this country.

We climbed to the top of the ridge to get a view over Killary Harbour. Connemara, on the other side of Killary, was spread out like a fortress defended by the Twelve Bens, an undulating horizon of peaks, dusky grey against a hazy sky. A curved body of fresh water in the distance was Lough Inagh, about twelve kilometres away. The lake was floating in mid-earth, between the Bens and the Maumturks. Clouds dissolved the mountains into a milky opacity. My imagination, fixed on Lough Inagh, brought it as close as the steely glitter of water in the fjord at our feet. Distance was collapsed, perspectives were flattened, as happened when Picasso took painting to

Cubism and beyond: things which in nature are at different depths were presented on a flat surface for the first time. By a similar affinity, Paul Henry's Killary pictures, with the same hazy opacity, reduced depth and distance to an almost abstract surface of two-dimensional forms.

We were now into the second phase of the climb, from a ridge at 430 metres, up a steep slope to the summit. The westward slope overlooking Uggool beach is an even, tight sward of sedges and grass without any litter of rock on the surface such as you often get at these altitudes. We stopped to survey the mouth of Killary Harbour with abandoned rings of salmon cages from a fish farm that has now been superseded by another farther out near Inishdegil. Fergal once went diving at the mouth of Killary and saw the whole seabed covered in sludge from foodstuff fallen through the cages. I indulged in a wild rant about the damage done to the environment by fish farming, forestry and sheep overgrazing, about how careless policy-makers had been about the impact of these schemes.

The little hamlet of Rosroe was visible on the other side of the fjord. I mentioned Wittgenstein's Connemara sojourn here and suggested that a poem about the great Cambridge philosopher at Rosroe was a standard exercise for an Irish poet. Wittgenstein's gloomy fixations now seemed irrelevant in the excellent conditions: I preferred to look down on Uggool beach with its fringe of turquoise water, and evoke Michael Longley's celebrations of the natural world at Carrigskeewaun, just a couple of kilometres to the north. This very literary corner of Mayo has been the context for Michael and Ethna Viney's long-running column in *The Irish Times*, and it also includes the biologist David Cabot's house: Cabot is Ireland's most prolific and authoritative naturalist and has published three monographs in the Collins New Naturalist series, including a definitive account of Ireland's natural history.[46]

The summit of Mweelrea, which had pulled me along past these literary geographies, was an anti-climax: the highest point on a faintly curved exposure of peat with a surprisingly small, loose cairn; at 814 metres, it is the highest mountain in Connacht, and the twelfth highest in Ireland. We paused to take a selfie, and moved on. As conditions were ideal, and I felt relaxed, we decided to take in Ben Bury to the north and follow a long ridge back to Delphi on the opposite side of the valley to our outward route. The ground on the saddle north of Mweelrea is more truly montane, a littered exposure of rock with moss and low sedges. A steady succession of swallows was crossing the col at 650 metres and – as if to mark this setting as montane – we heard a golden plover's lonely call and watched the bird covering a great sweep of sky to avoid us. Its solitude was threatened by several parties of walkers; we passed one group of four and exchanged cheerful greetings.

Here were variations in the rock: one outcrop of brittle stone was breaking up into thin slabs and fragments, the kind of stone used widely in south Kerry and West Cork for old huts and cottages. Not far away, a group of large, squarish blocks up to eight feet high were set in a huddle with thin bands of quartz emerging in relief from the surface. The quartz is more resistant to weathering than the rock in which it occurs, so it endures as slightly raised bands. The effect of these scorings of white in the grey rock was very pleasing and

I gave credit for originality and inventiveness to these mute residues of ancient processes.

Having passed the elevation of Ben Bury, we were moving towards the top of the great corrie at Doo Lough. The southern rim of the corrie emerged on our horizon above the northern rim we were following. The German word *emporragen* came to mind: it means 'to tower', 'to rise up', and suggests upward movement on the part of a cliff face, a summit or other structure. This upward movement is of course only in the mind, and the word is a good match for the subjective streak in German philosophy and culture. The domineering mind imagines that the mountains are rising up whereas the inert mass of rock is simply existing. Still, Fergal and I were awestruck by the size of the corrie at *Log Mór* ('great hollow'), and if I had to nominate a philosophical position in today's terrain I should infinitely prefer this theatre of wonder to Wittgenstein's indoor retreat in the cottage at Rosroe.

At one point on the corrie wall, we estimated a drop of 300 metres from the top of the ridge to the beginning of a scree slope under the cliff. Amazingly, there is a reliable path right across the back of the corrie: a broad ramp, with its own flank of cliffs and escarpments, takes you up in a steady diagonal from left to right, to the ridge we were on; we could see a distinct sheep track emerging at the top. Lugmore, for all its drama of scale, is safely negotiable by sheep's hoof or human foot, though I should not attempt it in bad weather and it could be a hazardous trap if cloud came down. It was here that the family of sea eagles described by Mrs Houstoun must have been killed. She describes their destruction in her book, *Twenty Years in the Wild West* (1879). A party from the estate climbed to the eyrie at Lugmore, took the young eagles from the nest and tied them to a nearby spot. She writes:

> The ultimate fate of the captured eaglets was, to be securely fastened in a nook within easy reach of their human enemies. Instinct, it was safely calculated, would soon lead the parent birds to the spot where their young had been conveyed, and, whilst ministering to their wants, it would be, and *was* an easy matter for the Inverness-shire herd, (burning with the desire to avenge the crime of lambecide) to shoot the splendid pair of eagles dead.[47]

To her credit, she did voice some regret at the killing:

> As a question of sentiment I was dead against the extermination of these grand aboriginies – these splendid "Arabs of the air." I loved to watch them in their circling flight on high, and then the sudden swoop landward to a destined prey was wondrous in its fell rapidity.[48]

The estate keepers had a double mission against these birds: one was to prevent them from taking lambs on their estate; the other was to save stocks of grouse and other game.

Matilda Houstoun was an observant reporter on eagles in her part of Mayo, and also believed that the destruction of eagles to protect game stocks was a mistake, because, 'Both on our own moors, and on those of Achill, where the same murderous policy had prevailed, the grouse, instead of increasing in number with the slaughter of their foes, were found to sensibly diminish.' The reason for this, she thought, was that 'stoats and weasels (sic)… gained immeasurably by the extermination of eagles.' In a similar vein, writing in 1876 about the spread of disease among grouse in Mayo, George

Roper believed it was due to the destruction by gamekeepers of 'the hawks, and kites, buzzards and harriers, which formerly abounded on the bogs and moors.'[49]

From where we stood, looking at Lugmore and its eagle memories, the ridge line was broken by two deep depressions, with a steep peak between them. This peak did not look easily accessible, but we arrived at the top half an hour later, having passed several other walkers. One group of six men carried pilgrim's staffs, Croagh Patrick style, and saluted us cheerfully; we chatted for a while in a hearty comradeship of the open mountain on that splendid autumn day.

We followed the ridge past Lugmore until it came to an abrupt end on a shoulder at over 600 metres. We went down directly from there, zigzagging our way on the grassy incline where generations of sheep had trampled the slope into narrow terraces, these acting as steps for our jolted legs. When the slope eventually bottomed out in the floor of the glen, we toiled through tussocks of purple moor grass to reach the river and the plantation beside the Adventure Centre. The rocky river (*abhainn na gcloch*) had a great display of flowering heathers along its banks, including St Dabeoc's heath, with its big pink flowers and white undersides to its broad leaves. Cross-leaved heath, bell heather and Calluna completed the set, with spikes of goldenrod standing here and there like sentries. The ground was rough, and in my fatigue I stumbled several times in the tussocks, but the track was near, and it got us to the car by 6 p.m. Nearly nine hours' walking today was my record for the year. We chatted to a group from Cavan whose day almost exactly matched ours, except that they had driven for three hours to get here, and were now driving home.

Annagh

September 7

I slept well, with just a slight soreness in one knee, which had eased by the morning. As the weather was still holding, Jessica persuaded me to make another trip back to Achill to show her the 'secret beach' at Annagh, above Dooagh. We delayed until the afternoon, when the sky was supposed to clear, in light winds.

We followed the sheep track across the bog leading to the old, rocky trail across the ridge. I caught a large grasshopper and held it up between us to admire its rich green, yellow and orange; its gem-like intensity was a signal for the interest the day would bring. Then, crossing the bog, we entered a silence; the unmarked grassy expanse was the perfect place to check our tinnitus: Jessica's had gone; mine was a slight hum that did not concern me. As we walked on towards the ridge, we approached another sound: the waves of the sea. Blacksod Bay appeared to the north; Jessica identified the tip of the Mullet, and I pointed to Duvillaun.

The trail got confused and dispersed on the ridge itself. We tried to start the descent down the other side, but there was no sign of the track. 'Keep up,' I said, 'until you can see what's underneath you,' a rule I learned on a bad day at Sauce Creek in Kerry many years ago, when I got into a very dangerous descent. Jessica disliked the breeze that was now stiff in our faces from the north; I pointed to the surface of Lough Nakeeroge below: there was only a slight disturbance, which meant calm conditions.

A hundred metres farther on, we found the old trail that

runs down to the lake and saw the bothy used by the lobster men couched in rust-coloured bracken on a shelf to the west. 'It can't have been all gloom,' Jessica said of these traditional people, and I thought again of the generations who crossed this ridge, their voices lit by gossip and intrigue.

By late afternoon much of the mountain above us was in shadow, so we hurried on to the western corner of the lake to stay in light. The sea comes right in to the foot of the moraine damming the lake, and we wanted to see if it was sandy, and perhaps swimmable. The shore we came upon was rocky. The only sandy stretch of beach was near the eastern end of the lake, so we tracked the moraine farther on to check, conscious that we were running out of time, and would soon have to turn back. A fling of dunlins rose off the moraine and hurried off towards the west, where there were other lakes to draw them down for the night.

I walked on, while Jessica stopped to spend a penny; she had just hunkered down when we heard engine noise, absolutely distinct and singular in this remote place. I could spot no trawler or lobster boat on the sea. Then a distant helicopter appeared, coming from Black Rock lighthouse – why else would it be crossing the western space of Blacksod Bay? Jessica laughed to think that military technology had spotted her with her pants down.

We had reached our turnaround time, so Annagh Beach was a trophy we saved for another visit. The lake water was not cold, and would be comfortable for a swim. I picked some dried lumps of otter spraint from the lakeshore and nosed their fishy smell. Unusual ripples and disturbances spread from a point on the far side: the otter must have been there, and had probably been alerted by our voices before we ever approached the lake. We tracked back towards the ridge, retracing our downward steps. Evening light had softened the mountains and ridges. When we reached the top, with a view across Dooagh to Menawn, the low sun had picked out all the white houses, like neat Lego creations. The shadow of Croaghaun was flooding quickly towards them, so I photographed the scene while the houses, Edward Hopper-like, were still stark in sunlight. The sky was clear, with a big moon promised: as the sun's glare drained from the land, the rock and heather of Slievemore had a settled tone, which everything else in the scene was measured from.

On the way home, the car radio played modern installation music: we listened to a composition featuring sounds from the rainforest. Tropical bird and monkey calls echoed in the twilight as we crossed Achill under a full moon.

Annagh
September 13

September was warm – warmer than mid-August – and I had to put off plans for a climb of Ben Gorm. It was beach weather, Jessica said, so we headed back to Achill and Annagh. We chatted to a sheep farmer on the bog above Dooagh, who pronounced Annagh, like Heaney's 'Broagh', with 'that last/ *gh* the strangers found/difficult to manage.' He and his wife were on the road beside their van as he scanned the slopes of Croaghaun with binoculars. I asked him if he went there these days. 'No. It's a young man's game. Anyway, Brussels has cleaned us out!' He told me that farmers have to go out there four or five times a year to round up the sheep and bring them in for shearing and dosing; there is no pen for handling the animals on the far side of the mountain.

We reached the top of the ridge in half an hour and climbed down towards the lake. The wind was southerly, so the north-facing slopes were sheltered, and I had a concern about midges. A pair of walkers appeared briefly on the horizon to the east, but they did not follow us down, and we had the place to ourselves. On this occasion we had time to reach the western tip of the lake and follow the moraine all the way back to the lake's eastern end. Finally, there was the beach, like a chapter in some story about castaways, littered with kelp rods and rotting seaweed, with an upper deposit of grey boulders sparkling with mica. The familiar, heavy thud of waves breaking ashore repeated a message that this place was real, not some made-up piece of scenery.

Jessica was first into her bathing suit and strode off to conquer this shore for the twenty-first century. I threw a yoghurt pot into the water to check for rip currents and I gave her the all-clear when it sat there steadily like an angler's float. This was also my cue to put on shorts and wade in. The cold water clamped my legs with a pressure approaching pain. We both managed a brief immersion before giving up, having measured this fantasy in small doses. I watched the glinting turbulence of mica in the sand around my feet.

The Inishkea men used to come ashore here one time; they probably bartered their famous *poitín* for Achill turf.

From here back to Dooagh is a two hours' walk: not too far by our standards, a small distance for people who were given time in more generous measures than ourselves, a commutable journey. Gannets were cruising lazily over Blacksod, occasionally deigning to fall into the blue water. One lobster boat appeared for a short while to the west and then turned back. We drank coffee from a flask and ate sandwiches. After that, like do-gooder missionaries of a new environmental sect, we scoured the top of the beach for rubbish and bagged a dozen plastic bottles to take home. Stonechats were hunting flies and sand hoppers on the rounded, wave-worn stones. I found a bunch of white plastic bands that someone, a fisherman, I imagine, had knotted together and dumped into the sea; I presented it like a trophy to Jessica, who put it on her head and posed with her new Philip Treacy fascinator.

The OS map marks a megalithic tomb just above the beach. I could make out only the walls of a stone hut at the spot, in a four-foot-deep grove of nettles and bracken: the nettles were formed in a neat plot beside the hut, marking the site of a garden where they had grown potatoes for summer. I sketched stones and bracken for a while and left the mysterious megalith in its cloak of bracken.

Jessica returned from the lake edge with an offering: a thimbleful of fish remains from old otter spraint, still smelling of something – jasmine tea, they say. She showed me another, fresher scat of otter on a stone, with a noise of bluebottles. The calm, dark lake, with its black stone margin and grassy banks in this corner seemed consecrated to a hidden otter god, incarnate only in his spraint.

We swam naked in the lake – it could not be as cold as the sea, we thought. The ground shelved so steeply off the moraine that in a few metres we were out of our depth; I did not confront my superstitious fear of the *péist* emerging from the black depths to swallow my frail pallor and instead stayed close to the shore. We dressed quickly, and kept moving to avoid the gathering midges. Here and there along the water's edge was the bright, red-orange dot of a rowan berry that had dropped from one of the trees along the far side and floated across the lake. Once in a generation, one of these will be blown far enough beyond the water to germinate in dry ground. Apart from some dwarf willow, rowan is the only tree of this terrain, and holds sway here in its lonely dominion.

Throughout the day I occasionally glanced at the sky to keep an eye on larger birds wheeling overhead: ravens along the rocky bluffs and gulls above the lake. The day was too fine to be troubled by thoughts of extinct eagles, or of eagles to come. 'The only time is now,' I declared, as we climbed the trail back to the top of the ridge. I felt liberated at having put the rumour of sea eagles on Achill to rest.

Ben Gorm
September 20

Robin Ruttledge mentioned the Erriff Valley as the last area in Ireland to hold breeding golden eagles, up to 1910. He does not say precisely where the last instances of breeding were, but Ussher's journal of June 1898 is specific:

A long established breeding place in the Erriff Valley, *faced south and was visible from the road* … one man now dead used to creep in and take the young and offer them for sale at the car in Leenane.[50]

Another correspondent of Ussher's, G. F. Ormerod, wrote in 1892, 'The birds have visited the same place now for 8 or 9 years and the same man has taken the young several times.'[51] This individual, according to Ussher, offered the birds for sale in Leenane; Ussher also believed that the eagles bred every second year only. He recorded breeding here in 1895; the nest was robbed again in 1898, and when Ussher visited in 1899 the site was deserted.

There are several fine corries in the Erriff Valley, but the only one that matches Ussher's description is the corrie overlooking Aasleagh Falls at Lugaharry, under Ben Gorm. All the other corries on the other side of the Erriff Valley face north from the side of the Maumtrasna massif.

I decided to climb Ben Gorm ('blue mountain') from the Aasleagh side, taking in the corrie at Lugaharry. My attention was also drawn to a larger north-facing corrie behind Lugaharry, which should be visible as the summit approached. The contours were bunched tight here between 700 and 500 metres, meaning a sheer drop of 200 metres.

We parked near Aasleagh Bridge and set out across the bog to reach the ridge at a point marked Letterass (*leitir easa*, 'hillside of the waterfall'). I thought this would be an easy hike for the first twenty minutes, but we got bogged down in large tussocks of purple moor grass, which doubled the time, and it took us a toilsome hour to reach the ridge. My mood darkened, the valley we now saw leading up to Lugaharry had the familiar marks of overgrazing, and I felt drained of energy after a frustrating start. *Binn Doracha* ('dark mountain') I wanted to rename this mountain, but Jessica urged me on.

We had to follow the ridge from about 200 to 600 metres for the main part of the ascent. It was a sharp arête in places, with steep rock faces on the rim of the corrie, and a grassy shoulder facing south. I was distracted, and slightly cheered, by calls of curlews from the head of Killary Harbour, where the Erriff river entered the fjord. As we climbed, we got a view across to the south-facing side of the corrie, where the nest site mentioned by Ussher must have been. The OS map did not indicate how particularly steep one section of the corrie wall was. Outcropping rock on one of the upper sections was gradually coming loose from an overhang, producing a broad delta of scree at the base. Just above this scree fall, a little to the left, there were two broad intersecting fault lines in the rock, which appeared as two dark channels forming a Y. Each of these long fissures had a ledge near the top, in both cases sheltered by a large slab or boulder. To my eye, either of these could have held an eagle's nest, although only one of them appeared at all accessible to someone who was going to 'creep in' and take young eagles to sell 'at the car at Leenane'.

A corrie like this acts as a funnel for the wind, so that it can be blowing a gale at the rim of the cliffs while there is virtual calm a few metres away. We picked these calmer spots away from the edge for our breaks, to look at scenery, or eat a snack. The mountains in Connemara and the plateau of the Maumtrasna massif were spread across the southern horizon. September was staying fine, giving perfect conditions for these walks. As there had been very little rain for weeks, the track to the top of this mountain was dusty and dry underfoot. Years of overgrazing had speeded a process of erosion of the peat cover, so that in wide areas the peat stood out like dark, isolated floes on pale, rocky ground.

After the shoulder at 600 metres we were moving on a rocky, degraded upland taking us gradually up to a cairn – the summit of Ben Gorm. We had now lost the sounds rising from Killary – curlews, traffic – so that the calls of pipits took the silence by surprise. A large flock of fifty or sixty took to the air as we approached the summit. I also heard a skylark, and Jessica saw wheatears. There was even a dipper here, which we flushed from a small stream at nearly 700 metres. There had as yet been no pinch of frost to drive these birds down to lower levels. I came upon a plant of devil's-bit scabious in flower in a nest of sheltering stones, and sea pink was also there, shaking its head at the edge of an abyss.

I stood at the edge of the enormous drop just east of Ben Gorm. 'Do you want to test your head for heights?' I shouted. As regards eagle sites, this north-facing corrie was unpromising: the strata of rock are stacked too neatly, like bricks in a Jenga puzzle, and do not form gullies and ledges. Only the elevation of this corrie has the power to make you giddy.

Once we reached the cairn and added our tributary stone, we saw another cairn a few hundred metres away at the true summit. I hesitated about going that far, but Jessica marched on, and I followed. Three and three quarter hours it had taken us, almost double my estimate of two hours. We took in the mountains all round: Mweelrea to the west, the Sheeffry Hills to the north, the Connemara mountains to the south, before starting our return. From this vantage point, the earth appeared to be nearly all mountain, dwarfing the valleys where farmers had managed to husband little plots of fields for a few centuries. I had had the same impression in late April on Birreencorragh, surrounded by the mountains of the Nephin Beg range.

The desert we were on had its own life, one we lingered in for only a short while, as we thought of the hours of walking still ahead. I dreamt about spending a night there in a bivouac some day; as Nan Shepherd reminds us in *The Living Mountain*, 'No one knows the mountain completely who has not slept on it.'

Ravens crossing the sky tantalised us on the way down because they can cover our three hours' walk in a clean glide of a few minutes off these heights. Jessica imitated their honking call, as if claiming an affinity with them. We stopped on the ridge overlooking Lugaharry to study the eyrie site one more time. Then we moved off and followed the slope down towards Killary. I tried to avoid the purple moor grass this time, but we still spent half an hour plodding through its growth at the end of the walk. The only advantage we had was that everything was dry, so we managed to laugh as we stumbled and struggled through the flouncy tussocks.

Glenawough
September 28

As Jessica and I drove to the Erriff Valley our conversation dwelt on mortality and the number of summers of active living we might have left. A friend, now in his late sixties, calculated at the age of fifty that he might have twenty such summers left, but now he wants to push that estimate until he reaches eighty; he's an active, outdoor type who does voluntary work with the Mountain Rescue Service, and he feels no need to stop now.

We turned off the Leenane road at *Doire Iolra* ('eagle wood') and headed towards the esker and its gravel quarries. The corrie at Glenawough was only partly visible from the road as a ridge coming off Maumtrasna: I promised that the walk would not be long or arduous, just a stroll up to 200 metres where we should get a view of the lake. We parked in a small section of disused quarry, the sandy banks of which were riddled with rabbit holes. A few bunnies scurried away through dried stems of foxglove. Ten minutes after leaving the car we had scaled the last fence and were climbing towards the corrie. The slope was a pleasant litter of large rocks where wheatears would abound in summer, but none was there. Instead, a snipe flew up from a wet drain and screeched, complaining about something we did not understand; then a large hare – eagle food – appeared on the slope above us.

I concealed a late-season tiredness by walking slowly, in lazy zigzags up the slope, through midday warmth. Our house at Fahy should have been visible from some point here, but the haze confused the perspective, and I could not see Fahy church beyond the corrugation of drumlins to the north. Then we came to the top of the rise and saw a wide expanse of bog with the first small glitter of lake in a distant corner. I had come here several years earlier with a fly rod and had had to splash and paddle my way through bare peat to the lake, where I caught a sooty trout at the neck of the outflow; now, after the long dry spell, the ground was firmer, but the sense of desolation endured.

The marks of a farmer's quad bike guided us up to a trail overlooking the soft, boggy floor. We moved slowly on this dry ground with the crags and ridges of Maumtrasna looming above us on our right. As we rounded the rocky outcrops, the lake gradually opened up, and we discovered heather, and a few holly bushes and rowan clinging to the refuge of rocky faces away from grazing sheep. In one spot, the bare, dark peat was decorated with red rowan berries fallen from a tree growing from a crack in a boulder. The knotty tree looked like a witch's broom whose handle had been rammed into the rock, and forgotten; its berries littered the peat like the scattered beads of a necklace.

'Look! People!' said Jessica, as if she had discovered something to relieve the tedium of this ruined terrain; she was pointing to the horizon at the top of the corrie. I counted eleven walkers spread out evenly like a row of Tuscan cypresses looking down on the lake. Then the trees moved as the walkers continued their progress along the top of the ridge.

Lough Glenawough is a baggy square kilometre in area, slightly longer than broad, set in a horseshoe of cliff, scree and steep mountain. The rock strata lie at an angle of approximately forty-five degrees along the western side, and this gives a succession of sloping escarpments, with some softer, green folds where the walker can scramble down to the lake from the top. Where the escarpments are highest, the rock is prone to come away as falls of scree and boulders.

I searched the slopes above the lake for possible nest sites, but what was most striking was how many trees and how much vegetation there was on the far side of the lake on its southern, north-facing shore. The slope here is such that plants have found refuge from the sheep, and shelter from the prevailing winds, so the rocky bluffs are seamed with the dark chocolate colour of deep heather. The southern face is formed of an upper section of cliff; underneath this are three further sections divided by green zones of vegetation; and at the bottom of the face there is a less steep, green slope where vegetation has mostly grown over wide falls of scree. Many of the trees had already lost their leaves, and they appeared in the binoculars only as thin trunks, producing a pattern of fine, silvery, vertical scoring on the corrie wall. Here and there, a large tree with its yellowish crop of leaves sat high on the corrie wall, marking a substantial ledge. The entire southern lakeshore was decorated with a delightful line of trees, spaced fairly regularly; in that day's conditions, the lake water along that far side was almost calm, while a breeze was sending waves, and their sounds, in our direction. My binoculars made out a single cormorant sitting on a rock above an exclamation mark of guano just at the water's edge.

We stopped to eat a sandwich and drink tea in this theatre of refugee vegetation. Many corrie lakes in Mayo have a few rowans along their shores, with long roots probing through yards of peat for some meagre nutrients, but the trees all across the southern face of Glenawough are a marvel. We watched more walkers reaching the top of the corrie; a group of twelve came down towards the lake along a fairly steep, but safe, declivity to the east of the wooded face. Their easy progress had the effect of taming the setting, making it feel smaller:

we could even hear their voices travelling across a kilometre of water. Jessica's bright-pink jacket was now a mark in the landscape for others to see.

I made notes on two dramatic sections of the western face, where an eagle pair might have built a nest prior to 1910. One fold of bare rock above a scree fall formed a dark recess close to the top of the ridge, where eagle wings might have settled. This site would have been completely inaccessible without climbing gear. A few hundred metres to the left, there was another possibility, also above a fall of scree and boulders, where a wild stream flooded down to the lake from the plateau above. Two rectangular rock faces tilted towards each other, with a green ledge at the base. I drew an arrow in my notebook towards this ledge in front of a dark recess. Either of these sites had a romantic, Tennysonian splendour, but there were many other options among the richly clad vegetation of the southern face, and they appeared so numerous, as I scanned with binoculars, that my survey was again defeated by sheer profusion.

The rocks here are sedimentary in origin, and were formed during the Ordovician period in the basin of the Iapetus Ocean between 495 and 440 million years ago. At some later stage, intrusions into the rock produced parallel bands of white quartz; when the rock later became exposed, as it has in this part of Mayo, and started to weather, the rock itself was eroded more rapidly than the quartz crystal, so that the quartz bands can be seen in relief patterns, as here at Glenawough. I marvelled at these white scorings and stripes on the greyish stone. In some places the bands at right angles to each other have resulted in wonderful square and rectangular panelling like a fashion design; elsewhere, white ribs of quartz appear to flow over the rim of boulders like miniature cascades. Across hundreds of millions of years, geology and weathering have produced these inscriptions in stone, which I admired with eyes attuned to the bold experiments of contemporary art. I think these formations would satisfy the modern nostalgia for an art that was innocent and oblivious to the corruptions of the human will; here there was no creative agency at all, not even that of the primitive sculptor, just a silent sedimentation on an ocean floor over 400 million years ago, a series of quartz intrusions, and subsequent weathering. I think you would have to travel to outer space to find a greater purity of form.

As we walked back, retracing our steps, three other walkers from today's parties overtook us, crossing the bog below. Young men, they were walking at a brisk scout's pace, and did not greet us. They crossed a fence ahead of us, and when we emerged onto the top of the ridge, they were nowhere to be seen, having vanished into the undulations of the rocky slope above the esker. Our own pace was casual and relaxed: we had not exerted ourselves today and lingered on the slope, with a group of ravens tumbling and calling high overhead. They were enjoying the day too, performing their half-roll manoeuvres in mid-air. Then they dispersed, and a few minutes later another pair flew past urgently in close formation, as if the happy part of the afternoon were over, and now there was some alarming business to deal with up on the mountain. The contrast between this close pair, whose quick wing beats were clearly audible, and the happy flock earlier, was as dramatic as anything in Shakespeare.

I set these characters on a screen alongside the quartz

striations in the sedimentary rocks. I have little idea of where these words will go, who will notice them, or how long they will last. In notebook and sketch pad, on screen and printout, I make marks, like the grainy deposits along the streams we cross on our ways out and back. Some depositions last no more than a few moments or hours, like names written on a beach; others make sandy soil to tempt farmers for maybe a few generations. Here and there a mark is discovered or rediscovered, like a runic inscription on stone by no author we will ever identify, of a bushel of wheat sold, a god honoured, a life noted, a person loved. I consign these marks to the great sea of meanings in our time and hope that some few might be spared annihilation in the welter.

October

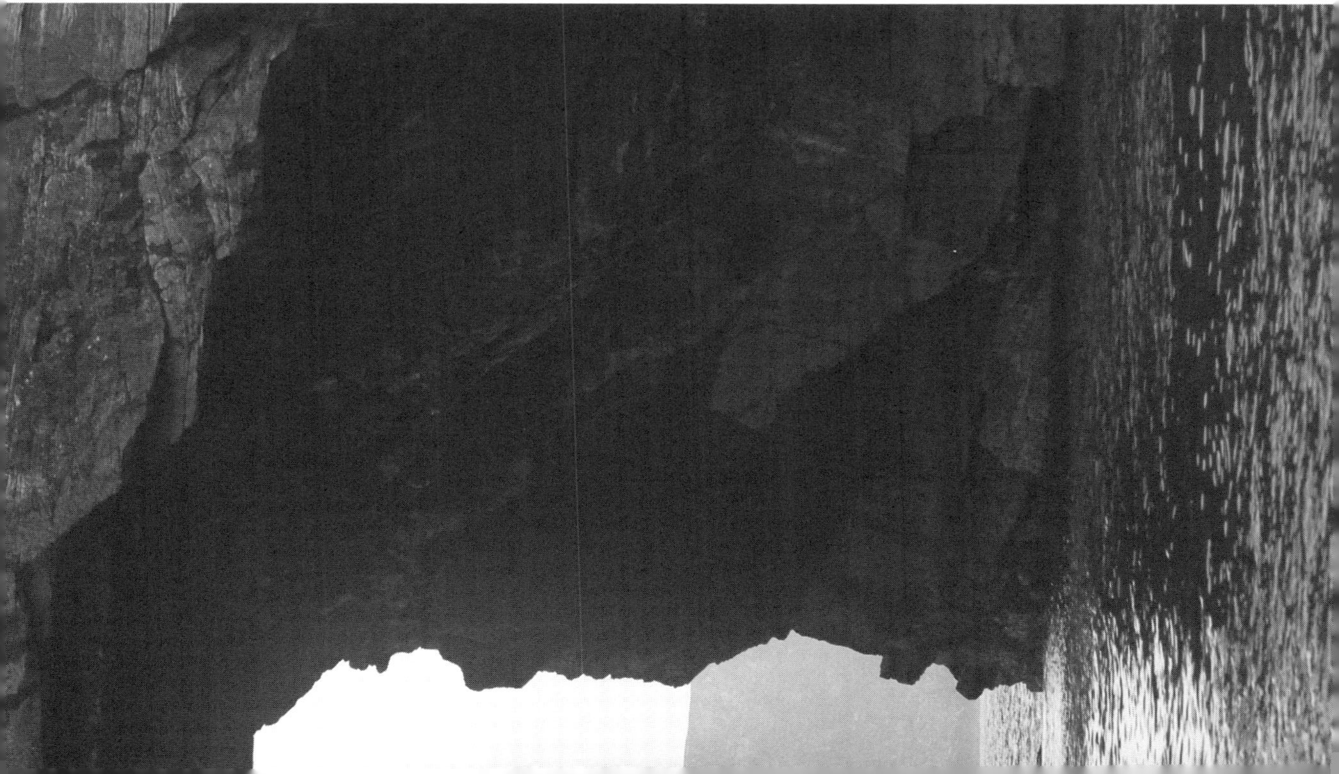

Ballinrobe

October 26

A westerly gale was bending the poplars; the gusts shot yellow leaves from the field maple in the hedge. We put the clocks back for the start of wintertime and at 10 a.m. set out for Kerry. After refuelling at Ballinrobe we were on the road to the Neale when a huge bird appeared in a murky swirl of clouds and drizzle, with a swarm of corvids in pursuit. I had to stop the car with the hazard lights on; then I pulled off the road to get a proper look. Jessica and I watched this bird through binoculars as it laboured in high winds towards Lough Mask. We were sure it was a sea eagle.

Twenty minutes later, engine trouble thwarted our plans for a visit to Kerry, so we had to turn back and limp home to Westport, driving through eagle country.

Donegal Epilogue

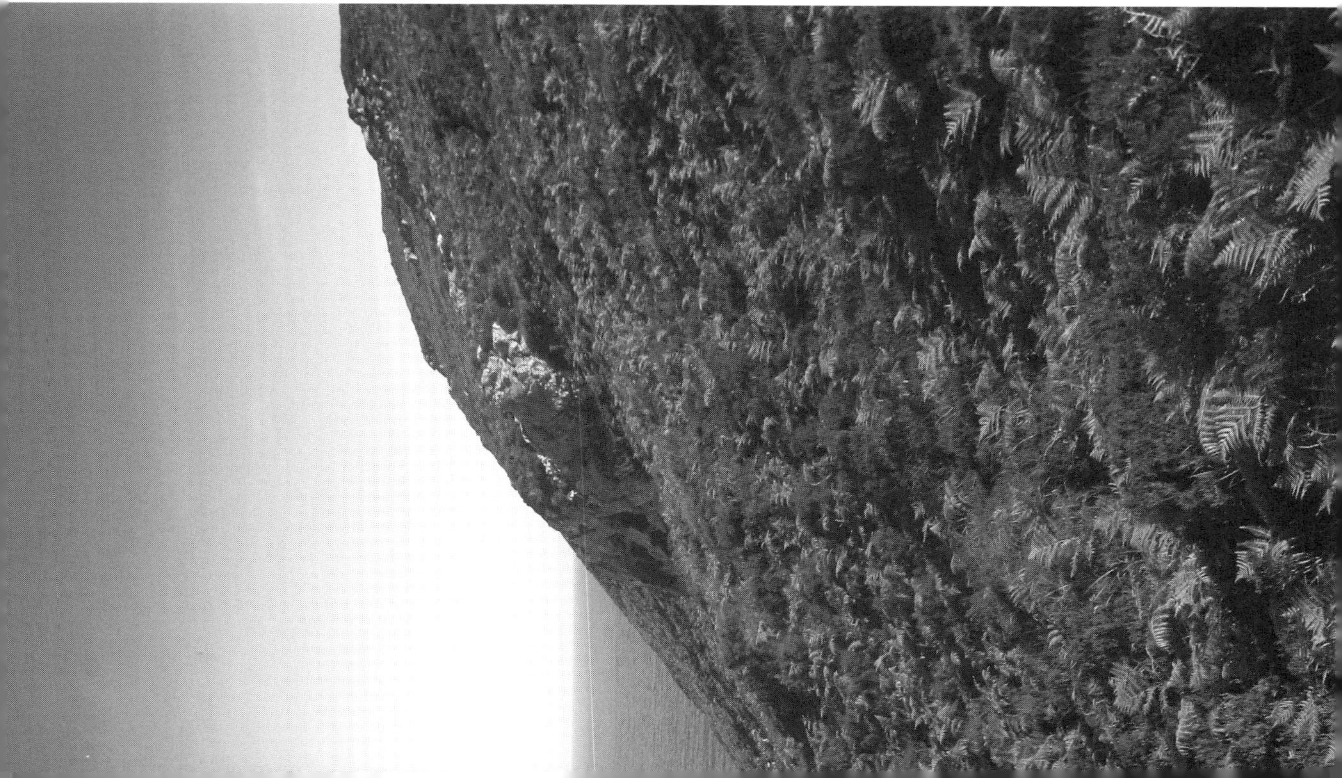

May 31

I first visited Glenveagh in the early 2000s to see a batch of young eagles in the holding pens, scruffy-looking, bright-eyed youngsters with wing tags being fed on dead rooks during their first weeks in Donegal prior to release. Glenveagh National Park in Donegal had been chosen for the golden eagle release programme in 2000 because it was felt that the young birds would be secure in the setting of the national park, with park staff in the area to monitor them. A few years later, I was back there with a group of students on a field trip and we saw two eagles flying across the glen near the castle, alighting on the mountain on the northern side.

At the heart of the national park, Glenveagh castle and gardens is a Renaissance fantasy beside a remote lough in the Derryveagh mountains, with a swimming pool on its own stone platform close to the lakeshore. The original Glenveagh estate had a harsh reputation from the nineteenth century onwards, but the work of a later owner, an Irish-American philanthropist, has softened the legacy. The Italianate gardens are crowded with camellias, rhododendrons, bamboos, exotic pines, Portuguese laurels and bay laurels. There are enormous terracotta pots with dwarf magnolias in the courtyard, such as I saw on a trip to the Vatican a few years ago; at every turn in the gardens there are urns, busts and statues to signify the neoclassical impulse at work. Many miles north of Garinish Island in West Cork, it is the same combination of shelter, a mild climate, and private wealth that has cultivated a dream of Italy on this site.

It was in the Glenveagh area that Arthur W. Fox encountered the golden eagle in the early twentieth century. In his book, *Haunts of the Eagle: Man and Wild Nature in Donegal* (1924), Fox describes watching a golden eagle stripping and eating a hare that it had just caught; he stayed in his hiding place for a long time, watching this bird feeding and preening. When it finally left to join its partner in the skies, Fox pronounced that:

> I had seen one of the supreme sights of my life. There in the heart of those desolate and lonely mountains, where the foot of man seldom strays, I had seen the golden eagle in his chosen dwelling. I had seen something never to be forgotten, until memory itself fades into 'dull forgetfulness.' I had seen the golden eagle in his dauntless freedom at last.[52]

Jessica and I visited in 2015, during eagle incubation time, and walked up the glen beyond the castle in the hope of getting a view of one of the pair that had established a territory in Glenveagh. The oakwoods were still quiet in early April; young hollies under the oaks lifted their burnished leaves to catch silver from light which otherwise would be lost to mossy gloom on the rocky floor where a few wood sorrel flowers had appeared. We sat at the old boathouse near the top of the lake, looking across the water at the tremendous cliff face on the mountain to the north, but no eagle showed. Instead, we were entertained that day by the calls of a peregrine hidden somewhere on the opposite slopes, and by a raven soaring across the blue, tucking its wings for a playful roll.

We took pictures of the Tuscan garden: statues of Bacchus and Flora; busts of Roman emperors; an urn on a column. It was a busy afternoon at the castle. A man with an accordion and a woman with an electronic keyboard played traditional tunes in the conservatory; families strolled about in the walled garden; a man talked excitedly to a friend about a falconry display he had seen there some time before, when a trained eagle flew down to snatch a morsel of food from a visitor's glove. The castle and gardens were alive with the public enjoying the legacy of a landlord and a rich Irish-American; everyone assented to an idea of style and privilege in an extraordinary setting.

In the visitors' centre, a stuffed golden eagle in a case carries a label, 'Shot at Bangor Erris, County Mayo, in 1915'. There is also a large photograph display of a climber abseiling down to a nest on a cliff, which reminded me of the peasant being lowered in a basket to an eagle eyrie on the frontispiece of Maxwell's *Wild Sports of the West*. We watched the video of the golden eagle reintroduction programme. The lady at reception told me cheerfully that the eagles are doing well, that they have spread beyond the Glenveagh district.

The truth is, the Donegal golden eagle population is now in a precarious position: in 2014 there were three nesting attempts with a single bird fledged; none of the breeding attempts in 2015 succeeded; a single bird fledged in south Donegal in 2016. There are currently about five pairs holding territory, and a further five sedentary, unmated birds, perhaps a total of twenty birds in the north-west. With sea eagles now secure at a handful of locations in the south of Ireland, and the species expanding in Scotland, I wanted to go back to Donegal to see golden eagles, and to hear about their fortunes at first hand.

I drove through heat, 'that foreign country', on the last day of May. Many fields were covered in a great yellow froth of buttercups, trees were high towers of greenery, and hawthorn blossom was piled in creamy heaps on the hedgerows. There is no better time than now, I declared to myself, and I posted this model truth on my Facebook page when I stopped near Swinford for a coffee break.

Ben Bulben appeared in the distance ahead, its great escarpment wall perfect for soaring raptors. I noticed that when you get level with Ben Bulben after Yeats's grave at Drumcliff, the mountain is not as extensive as it appears on approach: the famous brow is actually the point of a relatively narrow wedge; however, the less well-known northern face is just as imposing for its sheer, clean vertical. (Golden eagles from the Donegal project continue to turn up in these Sligo-Leitrim uplands, though none has established territories.) The limestone ramparts of this formation extend east into County Leitrim for many kilometres, and there are also smaller variations on Ben Bulben in sequence almost as far north as Bundoran, in south Donegal. One of these, a fin-blade of limestone dominating the flat surrounding terrain, somewhat isolated from the rest, is called Eagles' Rock (*Carraig na nIolar*); brown signs invite the tourist to make a detour to view it. I had paid my respects to this high altar of air and space on an earlier trip; this time I kept to the main road.

Many dark specks appeared in the sky as I drove and discounted them all as commoner birds, mostly corvids, even though hooded crows have a special interest since I read in Mike Tomkies' book *Golden Eagle Years* (1994) about golden eagles in south-west Scotland feeding hoodies to their eaglets.

Having checked into a small hotel in Letterkenny, I went for a stroll around the town after dinner on the last evening in May. A few thin wisps of swift noise and a late singing chaffinch were my only connections to the wild in this breezy town as a glorious month was ending.

Later, I turned on BBC2's *Springwatch* programme broadcasting live-stream video from a camera mounted next to a golden eagle's nest in Scotland; the screen in my hotel room gave me perfect close-up shots of both parents feeding a one-week-old chick.

June 1

Lorcan O'Toole had agreed to take me with him to check one of the active nests in the Donegal mountains. Our rendezvous was in a village outside Letterkenny, where I got into his van for the drive to the eyrie site.

As someone who has spent his career in raptor conservation in Britain and Ireland, Lorcan has a keen sense of the issues around the welfare of Ireland's eagles, and he has been close to the evolving story of management and mismanagement in the Donegal uplands. Although he has worked in the national park area since the start of the golden eagle project in the late 1990s, he is not an employee of the state's National Parks and

Wildlife Service but works for a charity, the Golden Eagle Trust. The trust currently runs three reintroduction projects: golden eagles in the north-west, sea eagles in the south-west and red kites in the east of the country.

We chatted about the fortunes of the project and prospects for the future; I was keen to hear about the current state of play, but was sworn to secrecy about the exact locations of active eyries: one in south-west Donegal, another in Glenveagh National Park, and the third is a site we were on our way to visit. There are a few pairs and single birds holding territory in other parts of the county, including a pair on the Inishowen Peninsula. 'A minimum of fourteen, maybe twenty birds in all,' said Lorcan.

When he parked later at the end of an untarred track, we stayed sitting in his van for some time, sharing stories of raptors, and their friends and enemies. Our conversation continued on the way to the eyrie he had checked three days earlier. I struggled over the rough ground of bog with peat hags as we entered a wide arena defined by mountain ridges, the bare rock glistening in the morning sun. The mountainside we were heading towards gradually emerged ahead of us, with an imposing cliff where the eyrie was sited. We stopped to set up the telescope several hundred metres from the nest; Lorcan was worried that the chick was not visible; the blurry image of white smudges above a rim of sticks was too obscure for me to interpret. Eventually, after a few more moments of suspense, he reported that the chick was still there. 'This bird should fledge,' he declared, salvaging optimism after so many disappointments. The lot of the golden-eagle watcher in north-west Ireland has not been a happy one in recent years. In 2015, no chicks fledged from three nesting attempts owing to a combination of bad luck and bad weather, and the population is now in a precarious state.

Despite all the years he had spent dealing with the persecution issue, Lorcan still spoke patiently and coherently about everything relating to it: farmers' fears, the power of the Irish Farmers' Association, changes in legislation, habitat management by the state, including its national parks, the gun lobby, grouse management, and – a theme he was increasingly drawn to – the future of small farms and farming communities in the western uplands.

We moved forward to a position on a low ridge about 500 metres from the nest. The horizon was the familiar yellow-green-brown of overgrazed upland, with glinting ridges of bare quartzite. A few red deer hinds appeared on the sky-line, while the lonely piping of a golden plover signalled a flat expanse of bog to the west. Crucially, there was enough breeze to keep down the midges.

As we kept vigil, I asked questions about the background to the Donegal project, which was the first of its kind in Ireland. 'We probably first started putting it down on paper in 1995,' he told me. 'We got Dr Jeff Watson to come over and have a look at Donegal in 1996. Then in 1999, we made an application for Millennium Commission money. We had intended to bring birds in in the year 2000, but we didn't get the licence to get birds from Scotland until 2001.'

The Irish project relied on taking the second, younger chick from nests with two young birds, finishing their development in enclosures, and then releasing them into the national park in Glenveagh, where they continued to be fed for a few months. 'We had always calculated on releasing seventy-five birds over five years,' he continued, 'fifteen birds a year, but we never ever got close to that figure.'

'So you've imported about seventy birds in all?' I asked. 'We've imported about sixty-six and we released sixty-three.' I asked whether there were any plans to release more birds, in view of the low breeding success rate. 'No. It became very difficult to collect birds from Scotland. The donor stock licence became very restrictive and it just became difficult to collect enough birds. Maybe because the project dragged on for a bit of time there was fatigue on the far side in Scotland because people were doing this in a voluntary capacity. We were not paying them. Whereas with the red kite and white-tailed eagle projects we had money to actually pay people to collect the donor stock, which made a difference.'

I pressed him on the issue of whether the population was viable, and cited the example of the sea eagles in Scotland, where a second round of releases was called for in Wester Ross, after a poor run of breeding from the first batch. 'I think it's a good question,' he said calmly. 'Whether it's in Donegal or a neighbouring county is another day's debate. If you were to do some population modelling, I'm sure you'd come back with the figure that this is a non-viable population; at the moment the figures just do not stack up. There are a number of problems down the road, not least that our oldest pair that's normally nested in Glenveagh are getting older. If you take the Glenveagh pair, that female was released in 2001, she's a fifteen-year-old female. By the time she gets to eighteen years of age there is a good chance that she'll stop producing viable chicks. It may already be happening now.'

I interrupted to check the figures: 'Sexual maturity is about four…' He pointed out that golden eagles breed up to their late teens. 'So you're talking about twelve or thirteen productive years?' I was disappointed at this, because my impression was that an experienced pair could breed for twenty years but my calculation was derived from reading about sea eagles.

Then Lorcan and I considered the prospects for releasing captive-bred birds, or for releases in Connemara or Mayo. 'There is also the option of going to Norway to get donor stock,' he said, as I got the impression that his main concerns now lay elsewhere: 'I think the real fix for the project is trying to fix the upland habitats to focus on what I would see is the real issue. The Donegal uplands are only a few management decisions away from being in much better shape.' One of these decisions would be to limit deer as well as sheep numbers because deer are contributing to overgrazing in the area, although deer are seen as an essential image of Donegal wilderness.

Another decision relates to grazing regimes by farmers, and as I listened to Lorcan's elaboration on this point, I got lost in a tangle of regional, national and European policies. Then we pondered a more general problem: the scarcity of broadleaved woodland in the Donegal uplands. I recalled the oakwoods in Killarney reaching up to 600 metres elevation, and many place names throughout Mayo marking the existence of woodland in former times. By now our discussion had moved from a pragmatic account of policies and practices to a wider yearning for broadleaved woodland: to bring more variety, more prey, and therefore more eagles.

Getting back to facts and figures, I mentioned how I was struck by levels of mortality in young eagles, and the possibility of feeding these youngsters during their first winter. Lorcan cited a statistic from Norway, which surprised me: 'Survival rates in Norway could be up to eighty per cent. Survival rates of Scottish or Irish golden eagles are between twenty-five and thirty-five, maybe forty per cent, which is deemed very low and unnatural.' He speculated about food shortage being an issue, but our discussion was still haunted by the threat of persecution. 'When eagles are young, they may be forced out of territories that are safe into a periphery. It's more likely that some of these young birds will encounter persecution or deliberate actions. Whether it's shortage of food in addition to that.'

This brought me to a question that I was reluctant to ask, because the whole story of eagle reintroductions in Ireland had been clouded by the persecution issue: 'How would you assess the poisoning threat to the Irish population of golden eagles currently?'

'I think that the use of poisoning is probably limiting the spread of golden eagles outside of Donegal. I think there are a number of young birds that have gone into areas of Sligo and Leitrim and maybe parts of Galway and Mayo that should have established territories and have not. So I think the limited amount of poisoning by a small number of individuals is still having an impact on these birds that wander over big areas.'

The problem keeps coming down to the damage a few malicious or careless individuals can do to eagles. On the upside, Lorcan cited the example of birds that had been part of the landscape in his area for almost fifteen years: 'We've had birds that have wandered all over Ireland and maybe there is more evidence now with the white-tailed eagles with satellite tags… so attitudes are changing, you can see that in the buzzard population and I would think that the golden eagle project has played a small part in the buzzard expansion by raising an awareness of poisoning that really was not there before the golden eagles were released.'

I eventually relaxed my role as interviewer and let Lorcan follow his own thoughts for a while. He did not see releasing more birds as a solution, even if there were questions about the viability of the Irish golden eagle population. 'Why are we at the stage,' he wondered, 'where it's non-viable? Sixty birds should have been enough. The bigger question may be in Ireland: can we not work with what we have to make it better?'

Finally, he brought up another development that may have a bearing on the eagles' future: a new release programme in southern Scotland, within sight of the north Antrim coast. He said, 'If golden eagles are released in the south of Scotland, I'm pretty sure the Scottish government won't let that happen without getting on top of persecution, which has been an issue in the south of Scotland. And some of these birds will come into Northern Ireland.'

I was left with the impression that the tide is turning in the eagles' favour, despite setbacks here and there. There may be recruitment from Scotland, and there was also talk of captive breeding of golden eagles following the successful rearing of a chick in captivity in County Louth. And as for the sea eagle, the population expansion of this species in Scotland is very impressive, making it a racing certainty that this population will spill further north in years to come.

Our talk of populations, policies and persecution had whiled away about two hours, without either of the adults showing. Lorcan then went off to check a merlin territory nearby where he believed a pair might be nesting, leaving me to keep watch. He was barely out of earshot when I crouched down to check the eyrie in the telescope and saw that both adults had arrived. (They were easy to miss at that range when they had landed on the rock-littered slopes around the eyrie.) One adult left and crossed the hill, doing a few 'shut-wing' dives, rather like a raven; then it soared up into the blue, gaining height rapidly in the warm June air. When I checked the nest again, the other adult had gone: was it sitting on a rock somewhere, looking at me?

An eagle appeared at about 3.30 p.m. in the sky above the eyrie, moved across to the left, doing more of those shut-wing dives over a rocky ridge; then it glided low over rocky ground to the east and landed out of sight, just behind a large outcrop.

The line of sunlight had now moved past the top of the ridge, leaving the eyrie in a large, oval shadow cast by the crag overhead. I was craning my head around, tilting it back to look at sky above the ridge, like an eagle chick taking in its new world. It would have another five or six weeks to wait and sky watch before fledging.

At about 4.20 p.m. the adult flew again, returning towards the eyrie, its head noticeably pale gold in the sun, like a female marsh harrier; it joined the other parent in flight across the rock face. They moved to the right to alight on a prominent, grass-covered rock: one bird was off again immediately and recrossed the face, gained height, then dived sharply, like a hunting bird, only to bottom out and land on the eyrie. I looked in the scope, briefly saw the adult, but then this bird faded out of my vision; had it left again, or was it hidden at the back of the nest?

At 5 p.m. I got my last view for the day: the golden-headed bird, whom I had christened 'Goldie', flew to the right to perch on the same green-topped crag overlooking the main cliff to preen. Then it was time to leave and rejoin Lorcan at the van; he had seen the jack merlin, but had not located the nest. I was effusive about my afternoon's watching, and we continued to chat about raptors on the way back.

June 2

I made a slow start after yesterday's excitement and drove back, on my own, to the eyrie site. On my way in, crossing the bog, I stopped a couple of times, as if observing a ritual entry into eagle country. As I came close to yesterday's position, I was conscious that my figure was an intrusion onto the eagles' horizon, and I regretted the bootprints on the flat, smooth areas of peat between the hags. They felt like a betrayal of the place and might lead another to me, or to the eyrie.

As I approached, I came across more boot prints: Lorcan's and mine from yesterday's trek, and then saw deer prints, the hooves much bigger than those of sheep. I saw no sheep here, and looked approvingly at new grass growth, at milkwort and heather, and the long thin blades of cotton grass. Then an old grouse dropping, and another, fresh, and one more. These signs of regeneration were encouraging.

I chose a cluster of peat hags for my position today, a little farther back than the site of yesterday's vigil: I was very cautious about disturbance. With the telescope I took a look at the nest, and could just make out a small shape above the nest rim, which I took to be the chick on which so many hopes depended. There was no sign of the adults. If they were on a rock somewhere they might have been waiting to watch me and judge my intentions.

In mid afternoon, an eagle appeared above the ridge to the left of the eyrie, moving east, away from the nest site; it landed on the same broad, sloping crag as yesterday, just out of sight. As if disturbed by the bird's arrival, a group of red deer, including a small calf, appeared on the skyline, moving downhill from that point. One of the deer paused for a moment in profile on another prominent platform of rock just below the eagle's position.

When the deer had dropped down on the far side of the ridge, out of my view, I saw the eagle again, heading back towards the eyrie. It stopped on a rock high on the slope just under the ridge line. I caught sight of it again at 4.30 p.m. going back along the same route to my left; this time it did not stop on the ridge, but continued until I lost it as a speck disappearing over the horizon.

I waited for another hour in the calm of the uplands. There were times when the thin note of a plover was the only bird sound. Then I heard a hooded crow in the distance behind me. Could its call be alarm at an eagle's appearance? When a sheep bleated on the far side of the lake, I reached for binoculars and discovered several animals grazing the slopes west of the eyrie, the first I had noticed in that place.

At 5.20 p.m. Goldie came back from the left and at first flew quite low across the corrie in a diagonal line. Then she turned outwards, her wings slightly upturned to catch the updraught, and in no time she was soaring overhead. Once she had gained enough height, she glided away to the right and was lost in the distance. I sensed that this bird was hunting.

I continued my vigil and was rewarded at 6.10 p.m. by the call of a hooded crow at my back: there was Goldie being mobbed by the crow, which then retreated. She soared overhead quite close to me, turning a few times to take a look. I got a view of her wing tag and noticed paler patches at the base of her primaries. She drifted off to the eastern ridge to do a few shut-wing dives, possibly a sign that she was not made anxious by my presence and was just advertising her possession of this territory. Eventually, she crossed the mountain high above the eyrie and faded away again to the west. A teal tinkled on the far side of the glen.

By 7 p.m. I decided it was time to leave, although I felt reluctant to leave Goldie to her patrols on these vast ranges. My step across the bog was lighter, my energies having recovered after the hours sitting or lying. (I had found an energy-saving strategy: if I sat upright near the telescope, the breeze was cool on my back, and it eventually felt chilly, but if I lay down in the lee of a sunward slope, the radiated heat of the sun was quite intense and I was hot.) I looked back a few times as the cliff face sank down under the horizon that I had crossed, and scanned the sky for a last glimpse, but the bowl of blue was empty.

I flushed a grouse from a wet, peaty trench where it had been preening, and collected a few feathers, a souvenir of eagle food.

While I was sitting in the boot opening, changing into my shoes, I looked up and there was Goldie again, quartering the ground I had just crossed. Her 'holding' attitude, tail spread and wings held kestrel-like, suggested that she was hunting. She wheeled off and glided briefly to the right, then turned into the wind to resume the hovering attitude; this she kept repeating, with a few vigorous flaps of her powerful wings to steady herself in the hovering posture. To the naked eye she appeared as a tiny point in the sky. Some cloud had swept in, domesticating the halcyon blue to more familiar Irish conditions. These were her skies now; she belonged there. I blessed her as I left.

July 3

I was driving to Donegal again to visit the nest site; the eagle chick should be close to flying, at about nine weeks. Lorcan had visited about a week earlier and had seen the chick with developed feathers.

July's growth had lost the fresh exuberance of early June and had gone rank in the ditches; a yellowish blush along the road margins marked the aftermath of mowing. Cattle chewing the cud of summer seemed to be reflecting on the past two months: as often happens, July was a disappointment; it was resolute in its own overcast, mild temper, rejecting the idyll of beaches, a dream it had exported long ago.

July 4

Lorcan and I drove in separate cars to the eyrie site. Cloud was low over the mountains, announcing the grey empire of rain. When we parked and got out of the cars, drops were already falling, but we determined to set out. We paused a few times to look at animal signs and we discussed issues affecting eagles, including disputes between individuals and agencies. How the vanity and intransigence of a few could threaten years of good, honest work.

Lorcan showed me a 'form' of sedge and grass pushed over, where a deer had lain down overnight, leaving a nest of droppings. This brought us to another topic: eagles do not kill deer or – only very rarely – deer calves, but there were instances of eagles, hunting in pairs, driving deer calves over precipices to their deaths. I mentioned an old story I had heard from the Ox Mountains in Sligo, where an eagle kept swooping at a pony, trying to force it over a cliff edge.

I brought up a current controversy in Norway, where eagles are accused of threatening reindeer stocks. One unproven view in the controversy is that there are too many golden eagles in some areas, leading to predation of reindeer calves; Lorcan explained that the nomadic people of the north, the Sami, have suffered occasional losses of reindeer stock. I suggested that if there were areas in Norway where eagle populations were leading to problems, surely there was scope for some birds to be brought to Ireland? The Norwegians, Lorcan told me, were willing to provide donor stock, but there was the issue of cost: helicopter flights to collect birds at eyries in Norway, and charter flights to get the birds back to Ireland. If transport costs were the only issue, with the Norwegians willing to provide donor stock, and no political obstacles in Donegal, then surely it could be done? Lorcan was still worried that twenty to thirty additional birds might disperse to areas such as Sligo and Leitrim, where birds have been lost to poisoning.

Perhaps in deference to my research, he switched the

conversation to the prospects for golden eagles in Mayo instead. If the supply of donor stock from Scotland had not dwindled five or six years earlier, the Ballycroy National Park in Mayo was to be the location of another phase of the reintroduction programme. Plans had even advanced to the point where they had selected a location for enclosures, to keep the young birds before their release. Now that the Scottish authorities were focussed on a new release programme in the south-west, with National Lottery funding, there was no immediate prospect of getting birds from Scotland. And this was where Norway might come in as a new source of donor stock.

We stood on the wet bog, with water dripping from our anorak hoods, debating the merits of second-phase golden eagle reintroductions, and speculating about the future for eagles in Mayo, whether through natural recolonisation or through extra releases. The rainfall had intensified. We continued towards the eyrie, floundering through wet bog, trying to negotiate as many grassy tufts as possible and avoid softer ground. With all the extra water on the surface, streams on the hillsides were showing a creamy white and a small stream we crossed on the way to the eyrie was vigorous and full. I wondered if such a stream were enough for sea trout to spawn in this high glen.

Lorcan then decided, 'We'll go to the nest. I go up at least once to check.' He gestured to me to be quiet and we suspended our lively discussion. Exposed slabs of quartzite looked as though the glacier had only just passed by, having ground and scoured the surface of the rock. I got out my telescope, now partly misted up, but there was no sign of the eaglet. In bad weather, birds could lie flat in the nest depression or retreat into shelter. There was a rocky recess to the left of the nest itself, which might offer respite from exposure on a day like this. None of the adults was showing; there was little wind with the rain, and an eagle would be reluctant to expend energy flying in these conditions.

We arrived at a grassy strip at the foot of the crag, about twenty metres below the nest. We searched for signs, feathers, prey remains and found none. The quartzite was sheer, and had the solid appearance of marble; there was no fall of scree under this towering cliff, only a small flush of stones from a stream coming down on the left. I felt an inert silence, of loss or extinction reigning on the scene and I shared Lorcan's worry that all was not well.

As I walked farther along a grassy ledge under the nest, stalks of wood-rush bent down to touch my passing head, each dark point with its own jewel of raindrops. The face of rock was richly decked with spongy masses of growth, and these dripped a rich excess of water onto the ground. I turned to get an eaglet's view of its surroundings: a vast expanse of deserted moorland stretching for hundreds of metres, simplifying the world. Life would be more complex for this young eagle – if it was still there, if it survived.

It was a wonder to me that a majestic life could be nurtured, could spring from such a bleak, forbidding place. Later, when I expressed amazement that a creature could keep warm and survive there, Lorcan cut across my eagle-pitying sympathies: 'The only question is food. That's what it comes down to. There is no disturbance, no exposure. The birds are hardy. It's all about *food*,' he added with emphasis.

July 5

I returned to the eyrie for a final visit, this time with a fly rod as a diversion from my eagle vigil. Again, I had to cross a wide area of degraded upland and felt anger at the devastation of these habitats by human activity. The early part of the walk was infected by my own agitation: I wanted to be away, to find a bonanza of sea trout within earshot of an eagle's territory. Squeaks from the fastenings and straps of my rucksack translated into calls of curlew and lapwing, which I knew were not there, bearing with them memories that could intrude on the pure gesture of the day. Fine drizzle returned as I wrote, seated on a peat hag.

As I came within a kilometre of the site, I saw two large birds above a ridge, a raven pair, which I interpreted as a bad sign. Had they moved in there in the eagles' absence? I set up the telescope on a mossy bluff at least 400 metres from the eyrie. The nest, clearly visible as a dark-brown pile of wiry old heather stems, looked empty.

Lorcan had said that I would hear the young bird yelping as it called for food. That meant that I did not have to spend all my time watching; I could cast a line for a while and rely on my ears to alert me.

Nonetheless, I kept checking the telescope at intervals, hoping that the eaglet might appear; perhaps it had made its way along a ledge and was out of view? But there was still no sign of an adult, and as time passed I became despondent. While casting the fly line I kept glancing up to the ridge, and at one such moment a trout swirled at the fly, but I missed the moment to strike. I thought it was not good to have your attention divided like this. The sandpiper stitched a thin seam into the afternoon, but that was not enough to keep me there. Still, the trout detained me for another while.

At 5 p.m. I stopped fishing and sat by the water. There was just enough wind to keep off the midges. In this setting it would be possible to adopt a Zen emptiness, to merge with the clear water and the pattern of the current, the only disturbance an occasional ring of rising fish.

Then I acknowledged my own need to let go, to leave that place of silence and desertion. 'And so my eagle searches end', wrote the pencil, eager to have done, to close.

Place names

The bulk of the place names in this book come from the Irish language, which was the dominant vernacular of the west of Ireland until the nineteenth century. The Ordnance Survey (OS) of the 1830s mapped the country and also set down standard English versions of these names, not by translation, but by the creation of approximate phonetic equivalents. These names are used to this day in common reference in English, which has now replaced Irish as the vernacular in most of the west.

Modern place names research is still uncovering details of reference which were missed or misread by the workers of the original OS in their brisk military campaign of survey. The names of the corries along the Corslieve massif are a case in point. Mayo is an area where many unrecorded names have recently been added to the legacy by the work of Fiachra Mac Gabhann, Barry Dalby, Uinsíonn Mac Graith, Treasa Ní Ghearraigh, Séamas Ó Catháin and others. These names are mostly from Irish, and can often survive, with their full Gaelic intonation and flavour, in the mouths of English monoglot speakers. Where these speakers are separated from the extinct Irish vernacular by just one or two generations, they may even be able to supply accurate English translations of Irish place names.

The following list gives some common elements in Mayo place names of the remoter coastal and mountain districts. The Irish (Gaelic) word is given in italics, followed by the phonetic English equivalent in parentheses, and the translation in single quotation marks. (These phonetic equivalents follow the practice of the early OS mappers and *are not* intended as a pronunciation guide to the original Irish.) The references have been checked against the standard source, Niall Ó Dónaill's Irish–English dictionary: *Foclóir Gaeilge Béarla* (Dublin: Stationery Office, 1977).

abhainn (owen), 'river'

ailt (alt), 'steep-sided glen'

binn (ben), 'peak'; sometimes refers to the brow of an escarpment or coastal headland.

carraig (carrick), 'rock'

cnoc (knock), 'hill'

coire (corry), 'corrie'

creig (cregg), 'crag', 'rocky eminence' (Ó Dónaill)

cruach (croagh), 'hill' or 'peak'

doire (derry), '(oak) wood'

dubh (duff), 'black'; can refer to a river or lake which is dark in appearance owing to the colour of rocks or to predominance of shade, eg where a lake is deprived of direct sunlight by its proximity to high ground.

eas (aas), 'waterfall'

fiodán (fiddaun), 'stream', especially a young watercourse on a hillside or on a bog before the water has gained sufficient power to produce features associated with erosion and deposition. Ó Dónaill gives *feadán*, 'watercourse, gully'.

garbh (garve), 'rough'; often refers to river courses or terrain marked by outcropping rocks.

gorm (gorm), 'blue'; often applies to a mountainside with extensive stretches of bare rock.

leitir (letter), 'hillside'

loch (lough), 'lake'

lochán, 'bog pool', 'small lake'

log (lug), 'hollow' [noun]

mám (maum), 'mountain pass'

scairdeán (scardaun), 'cascade'

sliabh (slieve), 'mountain'

speanc (spink), 'crag'

sraith (srah), 'level area', especially near a spate river, where deposition of silt, sand and gravel has resulted in improved drainage, allowing grassland and grazing.

strapa (strapa), 'steps in cliff' (Ó Dónaill), 'cliff ledge'

tamhnach (tawny), 'mountain pasture'

Notes

1. Reprinted with kind permission of the editors from *The Irish Poet and the Natural World: An Anthology of Verse in English from the Tudors to the Romantics*, edited by Andrew Carpenter and Lucy Collins (Cork: Cork University Press, 2014).

2. David Attis (ed.), *Science and Irish Culture* (Dublin: RDS, 2004).

3. Robert Lloyd Praeger, *The Way that I Went* (Dublin: Figgis, 1937).

4. I am grateful to Barry Dalby for these three place names from the Nephin Beg mountains.

5. William Hamilton Maxwell, *Wild Sports of the West* [1832], with biographical introduction by Colin McKelvie (Southampton: Field Library, 1986).

6. Caesar Otway, *Sketches in Erris and Tirawley* (William Curry, 1841).

7. John Hervey Ashworth, *The Saxon in Ireland* (John Murray, 1851).

8. George Roper, *A Month in Mayo* (London: Hardwicke, 1876).

9. Ussher Papers, 1:3.

10. R. F. Ruttledge, *Birds in Counties Galway and Mayo* [1989], revised edition (Dublin: Irish Wildbird Conservancy, 1994).

11. Ussher Papers, 2:60.

12. John Le Warden Page to Richard James Ussher, May 16, 1911, Ussher Papers, 2:60.

13. Richard James Ussher, 'Aves', in *Clare Island Survey* (Dublin: Royal Irish Academy, 1911–15) 31: 1–54, p.24.

14. *The Way that I Went*, p.197.

15. Tony Murray, Cameron Clotworthy and Andrew Bleasdale, 'A Survey of Red Grouse (*Lagopus lagopus scoticus*) in the Owenduff/ Nephin Complex Special Protection Area, County Mayo' (Dublin: National Parks and Wildlife Service, 2013; npws.ie).

16. Jim Crumley, *The Eagle's Way* (Glasgow: Saraband, 2014).

17. Caesar Otway, *Sketches in Erris and Tirawley* (William Curry, 1841).

18. Robert Lloyd Praeger, 'The Flora of Clare Island', *Irish Naturalist*, 12: 277–94, p.284.

19. Seán Lysaght, *Robert Lloyd Praeger: The Life of a Naturalist* (Dublin: Four Courts Press, 1998).

20. *Wild Sports of the West*, pp.100–01.

21. Tim Robinson, *Connemara Part 1: Introduction and Gazetteer* (Roundstone: Folding Landscapes, 1990).

22. Nan Shepherd, *The Living Mountain* (Canongate, 2011).

23. Fiachra Mac Gabhann, *Logainmneacha Mhaigh Eo* (Coscéim, 2014).

24. Richard Pococke, *Irish Tours*, edited by John McVeagh (Dublin: Irish Academic Press, 1995).

25. Mike McCormack, *Solar Bones* (Dublin: Tramp Press, 2016), p.19.

26. Máire Mac Néill, *The Festival of Lughnasa*, two volumes (Dublin: Comhairle Béaloideas Éireann, 1962), II, p.190.

27. Otway, *Sketches*, pp.306–07.

28. Otway, *Sketches*, p.323.

29. *ibid.*, pp.294–95.

30. A skerry is a 'rugged insulated sea-rock' (Oxford English Dictionary).

31. Coumasasharn is the setting for a memorable literary account of an attempt by two boys to capture young golden eagles at their nest. See Sir William Francis Butler, *Red Cloud, The Solitary Sioux, A Story of the Great Prairie* (London: Low, Marston, Searle and Rivington, 1882), Chapter 1.

32. Cathal Pórtéir, *Famine Echoes* (Dublin: Gill and Macmillan, 1995), pp.62-63. Otway records two other stories, from Erris and Kerry, of human kleptoparisitism on eagles: *Sketches*, pp.310–11.

33. *Wild Sports of the West*, p.101.

34. Liam Mac Coisdealbha, 'Seanchas ó Iorrus', *Béaloideas*, 13: 173–237, pp.205–06.

35. It was first described by John Bush in *Hibernia Curiosa, A Letter from a Gentleman in Dublin to his Friend at Dover in Kent, Giving a General View of the Manners, Customs, Dispositions, &c of the Inhabitants of Ireland* (London: W. Flexney, 1769). 'The upper lake standing about nine or ten feet higher than the lower, occasions a shallow descent of the waters… over which the boat must be drawn by the rowers, the passengers getting on shore, and embarking again above the shallow'.

36. See Carpenter and Collins (eds.), *The Irish Poet and the Natural World*, pp.276–77, ll.243–50.

37. Charles Smith, *The Antient and Present State of the County of Kerry* (Dublin: Ewing et al., 1756).

38. G. N. Wright, *A Guide to the Lakes of Killarney*, with engravings after designs by George Petrie (London: Baldwin, Cradock and Joy, 1822).

39. This waterfall was depicted many times by Swiss and Austrian landscape artists from the Romantic period onwards, and was also celebrated by Goethe in his account of travel in Switzerland in November 1779. The painting I saw over thirty years ago at the Musée d'Art et d'Histoire in Geneva is by François Diday (1802–77).

40. Robert Warren to Richard James Ussher, July 6, 1892, Ussher Papers.

41. *The Way that I Went*, p.190.

42. Otway, *A Tour in Connaught* (Dublin: William Curry, 1839).

43. William Thompson, *The Natural History of Ireland*, vol. I (London: Reeve, Benham and Reeve, 1849).

44. *ibid.*, pp.377–78.

45. *ibid.*, p.190.

46. David Cabot, *Ireland, A Natural History* (Harper Collins, 1999).

47. Mrs Houstoun, *Twenty Years in the Wild West* (London: John Murray, 1879), pp.104–5.

48. *ibid.*, p.105.

49. Roper, *A Month in Mayo*, p.105.

50. Ussher Journal, 3rd and 6th June, 1898.

51. G. F. Ormerod to Richard James Ussher, August 1892, Ussher Papers, 1:11.

52. Arthur W. Fox, *Haunts of the Eagle: Man and Wild Nature in Donegal* (London: Methuen and Co., 1924), pp.19–20.

Acknowledgements

I should like to thank my brother, Liam Lysaght, for inviting me and my wife Jessica on a trip to Norway in 2001 to see wild sea eagles in the magnificent setting of the Trondheim area. I owe thanks to the following for supplying information on the history of Ireland's eagles: Michael Kingdon, Chris and Lynda Huxley, Lorcan O'Toole, Allan Mee, Nigel Beers-Smith, John McHugh, Caitríona and Gary Hastings, Séamas Ó Catháin and Uinsíonn Mac Graith. My wanderings in Mayo were often enlivened by the company and stories of local people, and I am very grateful to the following for their generosity: the late Paddy McHugh and his son Paud of Tarsaghaunmore; John Booth of Srahduggan; Peter Bourke of Belderg; Michael Burke of Portacloy; Michael Conway of Srahnamanragh. Fergal O'Dowd was a cheerful and inspiring companion on several mountain excursions. Lorcan O'Toole was a generous host during my excursions to Donegal and he commented in detail on an early draft of the epilogue. I must also pay tribute to Jessica's enthusiasm for our camping trips and her heartening delight in Ireland's wild places.

Michelle O'Sullivan, who has been a valued seconder of this work from the outset, read the manuscript in an early draft and proposed valuable revisions. Chris Huxley also read and commented on the entire work, and Jessica proofed the final text with her usual, exemplary care.

I should also like to acknowledge several people for their kind contributions to this project: Cormac Kinsella, John Lyden, Seamus Lysaght, Yvonne McDermott, Maria McDermott, Eoin McGreal, Egbert Polski, David Reddington, Marc Ruddock, Jim and Howard Fox, Rosemarie Kiely, Andrew Carpenter, Justin Sammon, Barry Dalby, Paddy Bushe and Nick Harman. The maps were first prepared by Éadaoin Ní Néill of Aperture Web Design, Claremorris, and subsequently hand-drawn by Yvonne McDermott.

The epigraph on page 25 from Samuel Beckett's *Molloy* is reprinted with kind permission of the Estate of Samuel Beckett.

I would also like to thank the Little Toller subscribers who have supported this publication: Robert Goddard, Howard Wix, Claire and John Plass, Lori Van Handel, Patricia Millner.

Finally, I have to thank my grandson, Daniel, for reminding me that there is more than one way of looking through a telescope.

Little Toller Books

Nature Monographs

HAVERGEY *John Burnside*
LANDFILL *Tim Dee*
HERBACEOUS *Paul Evans*
MERMAIDS *Sophia Kingshill*
EAGLE COUNTRY *Seán Lysaght*
THE ASH TREE *Oliver Rackham*
LIMESTONE COUNTRY *Fiona Sampson*
BLACK APPLES OF GOWER *Iain Sinclair*
BEYOND THE FELL WALL *Richard Skelton*
ON SILBURY HILL *Adam Thorpe*
SHARKS *Martha Sprackland*
SNOW *Marcus Sedgwick*

Field Notes

MY HOUSE OF SKY: THE LIFE OF J. A. BAKER *Hetty Saunders*
ON THE MARSHES *Carol Donaldson*
DEER ISLAND *Neil Ansell*
ORISON FOR A CURLEW *Horatio Clare*
LOVE MADNESS FISHING *Dexter Petley*
WATER AND SKY *Neil Sentance*

Nature Classics Library

THROUGH THE WOODS *H. E. Bates*
MEN AND THE FIELDS *Adrian Bell*
THE MIRROR OF THE SEA *Joseph Conrad*
ISLAND YEARS, ISLAND FARM *Frank Fraser Darling*
THE MAKING OF THE ENGLISH LANDSCAPE *W. G. Hoskins*
A SHEPHERD'S LIFE *W. H. Hudson*
THE FAT OF THE LAND *John Seymour*
FOUR HEDGES *Clare Leighton*
DREAM ISLAND *R. M. Lockley*
THE UNOFFICIAL COUNTRYSIDE *Richard Mabey*
RING OF BRIGHT WATER *Gavin Maxwell*
EARTH MEMORIES *Llewelyn Powys*
IN PURSUIT OF SPRING *Edward Thomas*
THE NATURAL HISTORY OF SELBORNE *Gilbert White*

A postcard sent to Little Toller will ensure you are put on our mailing list and among the first to discover each new book as it appears in the series. You can also follow our online journal at **littletoller.co.uk** for new essays, short films, poetry and much more.

LITTLE TOLLER BOOKS

Lower Dairy, Toller Fratrum, Dorset DT2 0EL
W. littletoller.co.uk **E.** books@littletoller.co.uk